PRAYERS THAT AVAIL MUCH®
FOR TEENS

PRAYERS THAT AVAIL MUCH®
FOR TEENS

by

Germaine Copeland

Harrison House

Tulsa, Oklahoma

10 09 08 07 06   12 11 10 9 8 7 6

Prayers That Avail Much® for Teens
Revised Edition
ISBN-13: 987-1-57794-600-7
ISBN-10: 1-57794-600-6
(Formerly ISBN 0-89274-843-5, 0-89274-813-1)
Copyright © 2002 Germaine Copeland
Formerly copyright © 1991, 1994
38 Sloan Street
Roswell, Georgia 30075

Published by Harrison House, Inc.
P. O. Box 35035
Tulsa, Oklahoma 74153

CONTENTS

Part II Personal Prayers

Part III Prayers for Others

Part IV Special Prayers

A PERSONAL LETTER FROM THE ORIGINATOR OF *PRAYERS THAT AVAIL MUCH*

Dear Teenager,

If you didn't buy this book, you probably received it as a gift from a caring parent, grandparent, or teacher. However, the written prayers herein were suggested by your peers — young people who understand the pressures and present-day issues with which you are confronted every day. Teenagers from all walks of life are finding assurance, comfort, courage, hope, and faith as they pray from these pages.

You are living in a society that would lead you to believe that there are no absolutes — one in which everything you have been taught by the Church is being challenged. Male and female roles are changing, family values are in the process of being re-defined, and sensitivity to right and wrong is disappearing.

While educational textbooks, sociological theories, and philosophical reasoning are changing day by day, God's Word never changes. God remains true even when man's ideas, man's ways fail. Jesus is the same yesterday, today, and forever (Heb. 13:8). God will never change (Mal. 3:6). He will never leave you without support (Heb. 13:5). He remains a trustworthy Friend, Savior, and Guide.

In His written Word, the heavenly Father has provided us values and guidelines for living. These instructions are absolutes. The Bible gives to us "the law of the Spirit of life in Christ Jesus" (Rom. 8:2) — a life that has promised abundance in every sphere of our existence. It is up to each individual to choose life or death, blessings or cursings (Deut. 30:19).

During these years of discovering who you are, why you were born, resolve to decide your own convictions according to the Scriptures. Determine your identity, your integrity, your influence for good. Hide God's Word in your heart through Bible study and prayer.

(I encourage you to read the book of Proverbs — a chapter each day — over and over.) Determine how you will affect your world.

"What are you planning to do after you graduate from high school? Are you going to work, trade school, or college?" These are probably some of the questions that you are being asked. God has a plan for your life, and He will direct your path. **Commit to the Lord whatever you do, and your plans will succeed** (Prov. 16:3 NIV).

Not all the Scripture references at the end of each prayer were included in that particular prayer, but all of them may be studied for your spiritual growth.

I am praying for you and believe that you will be all that God has created you to be, and that you will fulfill His plans and purposes for your life.

Germaine Copeland, President
Word Ministries, Inc.

ACKNOWLEDGEMENTS

Many thanks to those teenagers who submitted prayers and offered suggestions. I also thank my friends, the editors at Harrison House, who worked on the prayers, deciding which ones would be accepted, lovingly editing them, and preparing the manuscript for printing.

Special thanks goes to Donna Walker of Roswell, Georgia, my beloved friend and associate, who revised and edited all our efforts. Her understanding of teenagers and her love for them are expressed in every prayer. She sees children and teenagers as individuals who deserve respect, love, and admiration.

Over the years, students have returned to thank her for caring enough to motivate them to learn, grow, and achieve. She is an extraordinary person, and a God-called teacher of young people.

HOW TO PRAY
PRAYERS THAT AVAIL MUCH®

The prayers in this book are to be used by you for yourself and for others. They are a matter of the heart. Deliberately pray and meditate on each prayer. Allow the Holy Spirit to make the Word a reality in your heart. Your spirit will become alive to God's Word, and you will begin to think like God thinks and talk like He talks. You will find yourself pouring over His Word — hungering for more and more. The Father rewards those who diligently seek Him (Heb. 11:6).

Research and contemplate the spiritual significance of each verse listed with the prayers. These are by no means the only Scriptures on certain subjects, but they are a beginning.

These prayers are a guide for you to have a more intimate relationship with your heavenly Father. The study of His Word transforms your mind and lifestyle.

Then, others will know that it is possible to change, and you will give hope to those who come to you seeking advice. When you admonish someone with the Word, you are offering spiritual guidance and consolation.

Walk in God's counsel, and prize His wisdom (Ps. 1; Prov. 4:7,8). People are looking for something on which they can depend. When someone in need comes to you, you can point him to that portion in God's Word that is the answer to his problem. You become victorious, trustworthy, and the one with the answer, for your heart is fixed and established on His Word (Ps. 112).

Once you begin delving into God's Word, you must commit to ordering your conversation aright (Ps. 50:23). That is being a doer of the Word. Faith always has a good report. You cannot pray effectively for yourself, for someone else, or about something and then talk negatively about the matter (Matt. 12:34-37). This is being double-minded, and a double-minded man receives *nothing* from God (James 1:6-8).

In Ephesians 4:29 and 30 AMP it is written:

Let no foul or polluting language, nor evil word, nor unwholesome or worthless talk [ever] come out of your mouth; but only such [speech] as is good and beneficial to the spiritual progress of others, as is fitting to the need and the occasion, that it may be a blessing and give grace (God's favor) to those who hear it.

And do not grieve the Holy Spirit of God, (do not offend, or vex, or sadden Him) by Whom you were sealed (marked, branded as God's own, secured) for the day of redemption — of final deliverance through Christ from evil and the consequences of sin.

Reflect on these words and give them time to keep your perspective in line with God's will. Our Father has much, so very much, to say about that little member, the tongue (James 3). Give the devil no opportunity by getting into worry, unforgiveness, strife, and criticism. Put a stop to idle and foolish talking (Eph. 4:29;5:4). You are to be a blessing to others (Gal. 6:10).

Talk the answer, not the problem. The answer is in God's Word. You must have knowledge of that Word — revelation knowledge (1 Cor. 2:7-16). The Holy Spirit, Your Teacher, will reveal the things that have been freely given to us by God (John 14:26).

As an intercessor, unite with others in prayer. United prayer is a mighty weapon that the Body of Christ is to use.

Have the faith of God, and approach Him confidently. When you pray according to His will, He hears you. Then you know you have what you ask of Him (1 John 5:14-15 NIV). Do not throw away your confidence. It will be richly rewarded. (Hebrews 10:35 NIV.) Allow your spirit to pray by the Holy Spirit. Praise God for the victory now before any manifestation. *Walk by faith and not by sight* (2 Cor. 5:7).

When your faith comes under pressure, don't be moved. As Satan attempts to challenge you, resist him steadfast in the faith — letting patience have her perfect work (James 1:4). Take the sword of the Spirit

and the shield of faith and quench his every fiery dart
(Eph. 6:16,17). The entire substitutionary work of
Christ was for you. Satan is now a defeated foe because
Jesus conquered him (Col. 2:14,15). Satan is overcome
by the blood of the Lamb and the Word of our testimony (Rev. 12:11). Fight the good fight of faith (1
Tim. 6:12). Withstand the adversary and be firm in
faith against his onset — rooted, established, strong,
and determined (1 Pet. 5:9). Speak God's Word boldly
and courageously.

Your desire should be to please and to bless the
Father. As you pray according to His Word, He joyfully
hears that you — His child — are living and walking in
the truth (3 John 4).

How exciting to know that the prayers of the saints
are forever in the throne room (Rev. 5:8). Hallelujah!

Praise God for His Word and the limitlessness of
prayer in the name of Jesus. It belongs to every child of
God. Therefore, run with patience the race that is set
before you, looking unto Jesus the author and finisher

of your faith (Heb. 12:1,2). God's Word is able to build you up and give you your rightful inheritance among all God's set apart ones (Acts 20:32).

Commit yourself to pray and to pray correctly by approaching the throne with your mouth filled with His Word!

EFFECTUAL PRAYER

...The earnest (heartfelt, continued) prayer of a righteous man makes tremendous power available — dynamic in its working.

James 5:16 AMP

Prayer is fellowshipping with the Father — a vital, personal contact with God who is more than enough. We are to be in constant communion with Him:

For the eyes of the Lord are upon the righteous — those who are upright and in right standing with God — and His ears are attentive (open) to their prayer....

1 Peter 3:12 AMP

Prayer is not to be a religious form with no power. It is to be effective and accurate and bring results. God watches over His Word to perform it (Jer. 1:12).

Prayer that brings results must be based on God's Word.

For the Word that God speaks is alive and full of power — making it active, operative, energizing and effective; it is sharper than any two-edged sword, penetrating to the dividing line of the breath of life (soul) and [the immortal] spirit, and of joints and marrow [that is, of the deepest parts of our nature] exposing and sifting and analyzing and judging the very thoughts and purposes of the heart.

Hebrews 4:12 AMP

Prayer is this "living" Word in our mouths. Our mouths must speak forth faith, for faith is what pleases God (Heb. 11:6). We hold His Word up to Him in prayer, and our Father sees Himself in His Word.

God's Word is our contact with Him. We put Him in remembrance of His Word (Isa. 43:26), asking Him for what we need in the name of our Lord Jesus. The woman in Mark 5:25-34 placed a demand on the power of God when she said, "If I can but touch the hem of his garment I will be healed." By faith she touched his clothes and was healed. We remind Him that He supplies all of our needs according to His riches in glory by Christ Jesus (Phil. 4:19). That Word does not return to Him void — without producing any effect, useless — but it *shall* accomplish that which He pleases and purposes, and it shall prosper in the thing for which He sent it (Isa. 55:11). Hallelujah!

God did *not* leave us without His thoughts and His ways for we have His Word — His bond. God instructs us to call Him, and He will answer and show us great and mighty things (Jer. 33:3). Prayer is to be exciting — not drudgery.

It takes someone to pray. God moves as we pray in faith — believing. He says that His eyes run to and fro throughout the whole earth to show Himself strong in behalf of those whose hearts are blameless toward

Him (2 Chron. 16:9). We are blameless (Eph. 1:4). We are His very own children (Eph. 1:5). We are His righteousness in Christ Jesus (2 Cor. 5:21). He tells us to come boldly to the throne of grace and *obtain* mercy and find grace to help in time of need — appropriate and well-timed help (Heb. 4:16). Praise the Lord!

The prayer armor is for every believer, every member of the Body of Christ, who will put it on and walk in it, for the weapons of our warfare are *not carnal* but mighty through God for the pulling down of the strongholds of the enemy (Satan, the god of this world, and all his demonic forces). Spiritual warfare takes place in prayer (2 Cor. 10:4, Eph. 6:12,18).

There are many different kinds of prayer, such as the prayer of thanksgiving and praise, the prayer of dedication and worship, and the prayer that changes *things* (not God). All prayer involves a time of fellowshipping with the Father.

In Ephesians 6, we are instructed to take the Sword of the Spirit which is the Word of God and **pray** at all times — on every occasion, in every season — in the Spirit, with all [manner of] prayer and entreaty (Eph. 6:18 AMP).

In 1 Timothy 2:1 AMP we are admonished and urged that **petitions, prayers, intercessions and thanksgivings be offered on behalf of all men.** *Prayer is our responsibility.*

Prayer must be the foundation of every Christian endeavor. Any failure is a prayer failure. We are *not* to be ignorant concerning God's Word. God desires for His people to be successful, to be filled with a full, deep, and clear knowledge of His will (His Word), and to bear fruit in every good work (Col. 1:9-13). We then bring honor and glory to Him (John 15:8). He desires that we know how to pray, for **the prayer of the upright is his delight** (Prov. 15:8 AMP).

Our Father has not left us helpless. Not only has He given us His Word, but also He has given us the Holy Spirit to help our infirmities when we know not how to pray as we ought (Rom. 8:26). Praise God! Our Father has provided His people with every possible avenue to insure their complete and total victory in this life in the name of our Lord Jesus (1 John 5:3-5).

We pray to the Father, in the name of Jesus, through the Holy Spirit, according to the Word!

Using God's Word on purpose, specifically, in prayer is one means of prayer, and it is a most effective and accurate means. Jesus said, **The words (truths) that I have been speaking to you are spirit and life** (John 6:63 AMP).

When Jesus faced Satan in the wilderness, He said, "It is written...it is written...it is written." We are to live, be upheld, and sustained by every Word that proceeds from the mouth of God (Matt. 4:4).

James, by the Spirit, admonishes that we do not have, because we do not ask. We ask and receive not, because we ask amiss (James 4:2,3). We must heed that admonishment now for we are to become experts in prayer rightly dividing the Word of Truth (2 Tim. 2:15).

Using the Word in prayer is *not* taking it out of context, for His Word in us is the key to answered prayer — to prayer that brings results. He is able to do exceedingly abundantly above all we ask or think, according to the power that works in us (Eph. 3:20). The power lies within God's Word. It is anointed by the Holy Spirit. The Spirit of God does not lead us apart from the Word, for the Word is of the Spirit of God. We apply that Word personally to ourselves and to others — not adding to or taking from it — in the name of Jesus. We apply the Word to the *now* — to those things, circumstances, and situations facing each of us *now*.

Paul was very specific and definite in his praying. The first chapters of Ephesians, Philippians, Colossians, and 2 Thessalonians are examples of how Paul prayed for believers. There are numerous others. *Search them out.* Paul wrote under the inspiration of the Holy Spirit. We can use these Spirit-given prayers today!

In 2 Corinthians 1:11, 2 Corinthians 9:14, and Philippians 1:4, we see examples of how believers prayed for one another — putting others first in their prayer life with *joy*. Our faith does work by love (Gal. 5:6). We grow spiritually as we reach out to help others — praying for and with them and holding out to them the Word of Life (Phil. 2:16).

Man is a spirit, he has a soul, and he lives in a body (1 Thess. 5:23). In order to operate successfully, each of these three parts must be fed properly. The soul or intellect feeds on intellectual food to produce intellectual strength. The body feeds on physical food to produce physical strength. The spirit — the heart or inward man — is the real you, the part that has been reborn in Christ Jesus. It must feed on spirit food which is God's Word, in order to produce and develop faith. As we feast upon God's Word, our minds become renewed with His Word, and we have a fresh mental and spiritual attitude (Eph. 4:23,24).

Likewise, we are to present our bodies a living sacrifice, holy, acceptable unto God (Rom. 12:1) and not let that body dominate us but bring it into subjection to the spirit man (1 Cor. 9:27). God's Word is healing and health to all our flesh (Prov. 4:22). Therefore, God's Word affects each part of us — spirit, soul and body. We become vitally united to the Father, to Jesus, and to the Holy Spirit — one with Them (John 16:13-15, John 17:21, Col. 2:10).

Purpose to hear, accept and welcome the Word, and it will take root within your spirit and save your soul. Believe the Word, speak the Word and act on the Word — it is a creative force. The Word is a double-edged sword. Often it places a demand on you to change attitudes and behaviors toward the person for whom you are praying.

Be doers of the Word, and not hearers only, deceiving your own selves (James 1:22). Faith without works or corresponding action is *dead* (James 2:17). Don't be mental assenters — those who agree that the Bible is true but never act on it. *Real faith is acting on God's Word now.* We cannot build faith without practicing the Word. We cannot develop an effective prayer life that is anything but empty words unless God's Word actually has a part in our lives. We are to hold fast to our *confession* of the Word's truthfulness. Our Lord Jesus is the High Priest of our confession (Heb. 3:1), and He is the Guarantee of a better agreement — a more excellent and advantageous covenant (Heb. 7:22).

Prayer does not cause faith to work, but faith causes prayer to work. Therefore, any prayer problem is a lack of knowledge or a problem of doubt — doubting the integrity of the Word and the ability of God to stand behind His promises or the statements of fact in the Word.

We can spend fruitless hours in prayer if our hearts are not prepared beforehand. Preparation of the heart, the spirit, comes from meditation in the Father's Word, meditation on who we are in Christ, what He is to us, and what the Holy Spirit can mean to us as we become God-inside minded. As God told Joshua (Josh. 1:8), as we meditate on the Word day and night, and do according to all that is written, then shall we make our way prosperous and have good success. We are to attend to God's Word, submit to His sayings, keep them in the center of our hearts, and put away contrary talk (Prov. 4:20-24).

The Holy Spirit is a divine helper, and He will direct our prayer and help us pray when we don't know how. When we use God's Word in prayer, this is not something we just rush through uttering once, and we are finished. Do not be mistaken. There is nothing "magical" nor "manipulative" about it — no set pattern or device in order to satisfy what we want or think out of our flesh. Instead, we are holding God's Word before Him. Jesus said for us to ask the Father in His name.

We expect His divine intervention while we choose not to look at the things that are seen but at the things that are unseen, for the things that are seen are subject to change (2 Cor. 4:18).

Prayer based upon the Word rises above the senses, contacts the Author of the Word and sets His spiritual laws into motion. It is not just saying prayers that gets results, but it is spending time with the Father, learning His wisdom, drawing on His strength, being filled with His quietness, and basking in His love that bring results to our prayers. Praise the Lord!

The prayers in this book are designed to teach and train you in the art of prayer. As you pray them, you will be reinforcing the prayer armor which we have been instructed to put on in Ephesians 6:11. The fabric from which the armor is made is the Word of God. We are to live by every word that proceeds from the mouth of God. We desire the whole counsel of God, because we know it changes us. By receiving that counsel, you will be ... transformed (changed) by the [entire] renewal of your mind — by its new ideals and its new attitude — so that you may prove [for yourselves] what is the good and acceptable and perfect will of God, even the thing which is good and acceptable and perfect [in His sight for you] (Rom. 12:2 AMP).

The Personal Prayers (Part I) may be used as intercessory prayer by simply praying them in the third person, changing the pronouns *I* or *we* to the name of the person for whom you are interceding and adjusting the verbs accordingly. The Holy Spirit is your Helper. Remember that you cannot control another's will, but your prayers prepare the way for the individual to hear truth and understand truth.

The prayers of intercession have blanks in which you (individually or as a group) are to fill in the spaces with the name of the person(s) for whom you are praying. These prayers of intercession can likewise be made into prayers of personal confession for yourself (or your group) by inserting your own name(s) and the proper personal pronouns in the appropriate places.

An often-asked question is: "How many times should I pray the same prayer?"

The answer is simple: you pray until you know that the answer is fixed in your heart. After that, you need to repeat the prayer whenever adverse circumstances or long delays cause you to be tempted to doubt that your prayer has been heard and your request granted.

The Word of God is your weapon against the temptation to lose heart and grow weary in your prayer life. When that Word of promise becomes fixed in your heart, you will find yourself praising, giving glory to God for the answer, even when the only evidence you have of that answer is your own faith. Reaffirming your faith enforces the triumphant victory of our Lord Jesus Christ.

Another question often asked is: "When we repeat prayers more than once, aren't we praying 'vain repetitions'?"

Obviously, such people are referring to the admonition of Jesus when He told His disciples: **And when you pray do not (multiply words, repeating the same ones over and over, and) heap up phrases as the Gentiles do, for they think they will be heard for their much speaking** (Matt. 6:7 AMP). Praying the Word of God is not praying the kind of prayer that the "heathen" pray. You will note in 1 Kings 18:25-29 the manner of prayer that was offered to the gods who could not hear. That is not the way you and I pray. The words that we speak are not vain, but they are spirit and life, and mighty through God to the pulling down of strongholds. We have a God Whose eyes are over the righteous and Whose ears are open to us: when we pray, He hears us.

You are the righteousness of God in Christ Jesus, and your prayers will avail much. They will bring salvation to the sinner, deliverance to the oppressed, healing to the sick, and prosperity to the poor. They will usher in the next move of God on the earth. In addition to affecting outward circumstances and other people, your prayers will also effect you. In the very process of praying, your life will be changed as you go from faith to faith and from glory to glory.

As a Christian, your first priority is to love the Lord your God with your entire being, and your neighbor as yourself. You are called to be an intercessor, a man or woman of prayer. You are to seek the face of the Lord as you inquire, listen, meditate and consider in the temple of the Lord.

As one of "God's set-apart ones," the will of the Lord for your life is the same as it is for the life of every other true believer: ...seek ye first the kingdom of God, and his righteousness; and all these things shall be added unto you (Matt. 6:33).

PERSONAL CONFESSIONS

Jesus is Lord over my spirit, my soul, and my body (Phil. 2:9-11).

Jesus has been made unto me wisdom, righteousness, sanctification, and redemption. I can do all things through Christ Who strengthens me (1 Cor. 1:30, Phil. 4:13).

The Lord is my Shepherd. I do not want. My God supplies all my need according to His riches in glory in Christ Jesus (Ps. 23, Phil. 4:19).

I do not fret or have anxiety about anything. I do not have a care (Phil. 4:6, 1 Pet. 5:6,7).

I am the Body of Christ. I am redeemed from the curse, because Jesus bore my sicknesses and carried my diseases in His own body. By His stripes I am healed. I forbid any sickness or disease to operate in my body. Every organ, every tissue of my body functions in the perfection in which God created it to function. I honor God and bring glory to Him in my body (Gal. 3:13, Matt. 8:17, 1 Pet. 2:24, 1 Cor. 6:20).

I have the mind of Christ and hold the thoughts, feelings, and purposes of His heart (1 Cor. 2:16).

I am a believer and not a doubter. I hold fast to my confession of faith. I decide to walk by faith and practice faith. My faith comes by hearing and hearing by the Word of God. Jesus is the author and the developer of my faith (Heb. 4:14, Heb. 11:6, Rom. 10:17, Heb. 12:2).

The love of God has been shed abroad in my heart by the Holy Spirit and His love abides in me richly. I keep myself in the Kingdom of light, in love, in the Word, and the wicked one touches me not (Rom. 5:5, 1 John 4:16, 1 John 5:18).

I tread upon serpents and scorpions and over all the power of the enemy. I take my shield of faith and quench his every fiery dart. Greater is He who is in me than he who is in the world (Luke 10:19, Ps. 91:13, Eph. 6:16, 1 John 4:4).

I am delivered from this present evil world. I am seated with Christ in heavenly places. I reside in the Kingdom of God's dear Son. The law of the Spirit of life in Christ Jesus has made me free from the law of sin and death (Gal. 1:4, Eph. 2:6, Col. 1:13, Rom. 8:2).

I fear *not* for God has given me a spirit of power, of love, and of a sound mind. God is on my side (2 Tim. 1:7, Rom. 8:31).

I hear the voice of the Good Shepherd. I hear my Father's voice, and the voice of a stranger I will not follow. I roll my works upon the Lord. I commit and trust them wholly to Him. He will cause my thoughts to become agreeable to His will, and so shall my plans be established and succeed (John 10:27, Prov. 16:3).

I am a world overcomer because I am born of God. I represent the Father and Jesus well. I am a useful member in the Body of Christ. I am His workmanship recreated in Christ Jesus. My Father God is all the while effectually at work in me both to will and do His good pleasure (1 John 5:4,5, Eph. 2:10, Phil. 2:13).

I let the Word dwell in me richly. He who began a good work in me will continue until the day of Christ (Col. 3:16, Phil. 1:6).

Part I

DAILY PRAYERS

—1—

COMMITMENT TO THE LORD

Father, I pray that Your plan for my life will be accomplished. My number one priority is to submit myself in love to You. I choose to embrace Your truth rather than the basic principles of this world. I will not be conformed to the pattern of this world, but I ask to be transformed by the renewing of my mind. Then I will be able to test and approve what Your will is for me. I believe in Your Word, which is Your expressed Will for my life.

Father, I purpose to obey You and remain in Your love. I love others and will show them by my actions. I commit and dedicate my whole body, mind, and spirit to You. I will serve You, my God, and keep Your commandments.

I will not follow the voice of a stranger. I choose my companions and friends carefully, according to Your

Word, and determine to walk in paths of righteousness for Your name's sake.

Thank You that You chose me — actually picked me out for Yourself as Your own child — to be holy and blameless in Your sight.

I have made the decision to follow You as long as I live. I trust You to lead me and guide me through Your Word with the Holy Spirit as my Helper. I commit and trust my works to You — so that You cause my plans to be established and succeed.

In Jesus' name I pray. Amen.

SCRIPTURE REFERENCES

Psalm 23:3 AMP	John 14:16 AMP
Psalm 37:4,5	Acts 17:24,27,28
Psalm 42:1	Romans 12:2
Proverbs 16:3 AMP	Romans 8:14,26

Jeremiah 29:13	1 Corinthians 15:33 AMP
Jeremiah 42:6	Ephesians 1:4 AMP
Lamentations 3:25	Colossians 1:9
Luke 10:27	Colossians 2:20-22
John 10:5	Colossians 3:1-3

—2—

PRAISE AND THANKSGIVING

Father, I love You and I praise You. I thank You for Your goodness and Your love. I'll continually thank You for Your mercy, which endures forever.

I praise You, Lord, and I will not forget all Your benefits. Thank You for forgiving my sins and for healing all my diseases. You fill my life with good things.

Father, You created the heavens, the earth, the sea, and everything in them. Thank You for making me so I can enjoy life to the fullest. This is the day that You have made and I rejoice, and I am glad in it. You are my strength and my joy.

I thank You and praise You for supplying and providing everything I need. You are all-powerful, You know everything, and You are everywhere. Thank You for being such a loving Father to me and giving Jesus to be my Savior, Lord, and Friend. Thank You for sending the Holy Spirit to fill me, guide me, comfort me, and teach me the right things to do.

I'll praise You in everything.

In Jesus' name I pray. Amen.

SCRIPTURE REFERENCES

Nehemiah 8:10	Psalm 103:2,3,5,8
Psalm 18:30	Psalm 106:1
Psalm 24:1	Psalm 118:24
Psalm 28:7	Psalm 136:1
Psalm 34:1	John 10:10
Psalm 48:1	John 14:16 AMP
Psalm 63:3-5	Philippians 4:19
Psalm 71:8	Revelation 4:8,11

— 3 —

WISDOM AND GOD'S WILL

Heavenly Father, may I be filled with the clear knowledge of Your will in all wisdom and understanding. I know that Your will and Your Word agree. I will continue to meditate on Your Word so I can know Your plan and Your purpose for this season in my life. I want to live in a way that is worthy of You and fully pleasing to You. I believe You will cause my thoughts to agree with Your will so that I may be fruitful in every good work.

Your wisdom is pure and full of compassion. I ask You that I may develop in love. I can be strong in faith. Your words contain a wealth of wisdom.

As for this situation today, I thank You for Your wisdom in knowing the right thing to do and to say. I have decided to listen to You. Teach me the way that You want me to go. Thank You for counseling me and watching carefully over me. Thank You for the Holy Spirit; He is my Teacher, Helper, and Guide. I believe He is active in my life.

I won't be afraid or confused, because Your Word brings me light and understanding. Although there are many voices in the world, I will follow the voice of my Shepherd.

Thank You for the wise parents, teachers, and pastors You have put in my life. They are people whom You can use to teach and instruct me. I will seek godly counsel from them. When I need to make an important, final decision, I will follow the peace that comes from knowing Your Word.

I dedicate everything I do to You, knowing that my plans will succeed. I will trust You with my life and everything in it. I thank You that to follow after You is to follow after peace in my heart. I thank You for Your wisdom.

In Jesus' name I pray. Amen.

SCRIPTURE REFERENCES

Joshua 1:9	John 10:15
Psalm 16:7	1 Corinthians 14:33 KJV
Psalm 32:8	Ephesians 5:15
Psalm 118:8	Colossians 1:9
Psalm 119:99,130,133	Colossians 3:16
Proverbs 2:6	James 1:5,6
Proverbs 6:20-23	James 3:17
Proverbs 16:3,9 AMP	1 John 5:14,15
Proverbs 19:21	

—4—

PRIORITIES

Father, help me to set my priorities in the right order. I commit to love You, and to love myself and others the way You do. Your Word says that when I put You first, everything else that I need and desire will be given to me.

Please help me to obey my parents in the Lord. I love and cherish my family. I commit to walk in love even when I am tempted to get mad or rebel.

Help me to put school, work, and church in the right perspective. I desire to be faithful, diligent, disciplined, and consistent in all I do.

I desire to plan my activities and work for You. When I put You first, I can be successful at whatever I do.

Jesus came that I might have life, and have it to the fullest. I will learn to have a good time by meeting people, laughing, and doing fun things. I believe that by putting You first, and by keeping all my priorities in the right order, I will have peace.

Thank You, Father, for helping me to set up my priorities.

In Jesus' name I pray. Amen.

SCRIPTURE REFERENCES

Joshua 1:7,8	Matthew 6:33
Psalm 1:2,3	Luke 10:27
Psalm 37:4	John 10:10
Proverbs 3:5,6	Colossians 3:20
Proverbs 4:7,8	

—5—

PROTECTION

Father, You are my stronghold and my fortress. You are my God; in You will I trust. I will not be afraid of any terror by day or night, for You are always with me.

Lord, You are a shield about me to protect me. You are my light and my salvation — whom shall I fear? You are the stronghold of my life — of whom shall I be afraid? When evil men come to destroy me, they will stumble and fall!

I can have peace in my heart because perfect love casts out all fear. You have not given me a spirit of fear, but of power and of love and of a sound mind.

Your Word promises me that no evil will come upon me, no accident will overtake me, and no disease or tragedy will come near my home. And You have promised me that no weapon aimed at me will succeed.

So I will be strong, courageous, and fearless. Thank You for angels to keep me safe in all that I do.

Father, You have promised Your children a sweet, peaceful sleep, so I thank You that I can rest at night free from fear or nightmares. You give me peace and rest; Jesus is my safety. Thank You for protecting me.

In Jesus' name I pray. Amen.

To remind yourself of God's protection,
read Psalm 91 and Psalm 23 often.

SCRIPTURE REFERENCES

Psalm 3:3	Psalm 91:5,9-12
Psalm 4:8	Isaiah 54:17
Psalm 23:4	2 Timothy 1:7 KJV
Psalm 27:1,2	1 John 3:8
Psalm 34:7 AMP	1 John 4:18

—6—

HEALING

I come to Your throne boldly in faith to receive my healing. I confess Your Word, believing that Your Word will not return to You void, but will accomplish what it says it will. Thank You for Jesus Who took my sicknesses, and carried away my diseases. Because of the stripes on Jesus' back, I believe that I am healed.

Jesus saved me from the curse of sickness. I have confidence in the Word which abides in me to heal me. I have on the whole armor of God, and the shield of faith protects me from all the fiery darts of the wicked one.

Healing is the children's bread, and I am Your child, so I receive total and complete healing for my body and mind. My faith is based on Jesus, the Word of God. Your Word is health, life, and medicine to my whole body.

Father, Your Word says that my tongue has the power of life and death; therefore I speak words filled with faith, hope, life, and health. I stand delivered to perfect soundness of mind and wholeness in body and spirit from the deepest parts of my nature in my immortal spirit even to the joints and marrow of my bones.

In Jesus' name I pray. Amen.

SCRIPTURE REFERENCES

Exodus 15:26	Matthew 18:18
Psalm 91:2	Mark 7:27
Psalm 103:3	John 1:14
Psalm 107:2	Acts 10:38 KJV
Proverbs 3:8	Galatians 3:13
Proverbs 4:20-22	Ephesians 6:11,16 KJV
Proverbs 18:21	Hebrews 4:12,16
Isaiah 53:5	1 Peter 2:24
Isaiah 55:11	

— 7 —

FINANCES

Father, thank You for being my Source. Everything that is good comes from You. Before I even ask, You know my financial needs. You said that the things I desire (in accordance with Your will) will be given to me if I ask You. Because I trust You, I ask specifically for $ _____ to meet my present financial need.

I know that You use jobs, parents, friends, or associates to bless me financially. I will cherish and respect those who bless me, but I will still recognize You as my Source. I won't worry, because I have You to provide for my every financial need. Your Word says that You take pleasure in the prosperity of Your servant.

Because You have given me the ability to obtain wealth, I will look for good ideas and opportunities to earn the money that I need. I will keep a good attitude and work hard. Thank You for giving me favor with others.

Your Word promises that since I have given my tithes and offerings to You cheerfully, without complaining, I will always have enough. I will stay faithful and thankful to You and to the people You use to meet my needs. Because I am Your child, I believe You will bless those who bless me.

Please help me to learn to handle my money wisely. Thank You for meeting my financial needs so that I can prosper and enjoy life to the fullest.

In Jesus' name I pray. Amen.

SCRIPTURE REFERENCES

Genesis 12:2,3	Ecclesiastes 5:19
Numbers 23:19	Isaiah 65:24
Deuteronomy 8:18	Malachi 3:10,11 KJV

Deuteronomy 28:1-13	Matthew 6:32,33
Psalm 23:1	Luke 6:38
Psalm 34:10	2 Corinthians 9:7
Psalm 35:27 KJV	Philippians 4:19
Proverbs 3:4,9,10	James 1:17
Proverbs 10:4	1 John 5:14,15

— 8 —

CONTROLLING YOUR THOUGHTS/ RENEWING YOUR MIND

Father, You know all of my thoughts and the attitudes of my heart. May my spoken words and unspoken thoughts be pleasing in Your sight, O Lord, my Rock and my Redeemer.

You gave me Your Word as a weapon to fight impure and unholy thoughts. Your Word is alive and more powerful than any weapon known to man; it is able to pull down all evil strongholds.

I will concentrate on truth, goodness, and righteousness. I will think about things that are pure and lovely, and dwell on the good attributes in others. I will think about all that I can praise You for and be glad about.

I thank You for giving me the helmet of salvation to guard my mind. As I commit to stay in Your Word daily,

I will begin to think more and more like You, Father. I will diligently guard my mind and heart by not allowing unhealthy thoughts to control me.

Thank You for giving me the mind of Christ. Help me to make all my thoughts obedient to Jesus, the Word.

In Jesus' name I pray. Amen.

SCRIPTURE REFERENCES

Psalm 19:14 TLB	1 Corinthians 2:16
Psalm 94:11	2 Corinthians 10:3-5 KJV
Psalm 139:2-4,23	Ephesians 6:17
Proverbs 4:23	Philippians 4:6-8
Isaiah 26:3 KJV	Colossians 3:2
Isaiah 55:8,9	Hebrews 4:12

—9—

CONTROLLING YOUR TONGUE

Father, Your Word says in Proverbs 17:27,28 (AMP), He who has knowledge spares his words, and a man of understanding has a cool spirit. Even a fool when he holds his peace is considered wise; when he closes his lips he is esteemed a man of understanding. Proverbs 29:20 (KJV) also says, Seest thou a man that is hasty in his words? there is more hope of a fool than of him. And James 3:2 (KJV) says, For in many things we offend all. If any man offend not in word, the same is a perfect man, and able also to bridle the whole body.

Lord, You have said that life and death are in the power of the tongue, and that I will be satisfied by the fruit of my lips. Out of the abundance of my heart, my mouth speaks. I will feed my spirit on Your Word so that Your Word will be in abundance in me.

Your words are life to those who find them and health to all their flesh.

When I speak Your Word, Father, it produces life and health in me. I will speak faith-filled words. I believe that I can control what I say because no temptations come to me that are unique or new, but You are faithful, and You will make a way of escape when I am tempted to sin with my mouth. Thank You, Father, for that escape. I will learn to be quick to hear and slow to speak.

Jesus said that I would be judged for all empty and idle words. Either I can speak words of love, faith, and hope, or I can speak words filled with doubt, unbelief, and hate. I choose to speak Your Word, Father — words of life, peace, joy, and faith.

Because I know that good words are sweet to hear and they bring life to people, help me always to be someone who says good things. Thank You, Father, for a pure heart and pure words.

In Jesus' name I pray. Amen.

SCRIPTURE REFERENCES

Proverbs 4:20-22 KJV	Matthew 12:34 KJV
Proverbs 10:19	Matthew 12:36 TLB
Proverbs 16:24	1 Corinthians 10:13 AMP
Proverbs 17:9	Ephesians 4:25,29
Proverbs 18:21	James 1:19
Matthew 5:8	James 4:11

Part II

PERSONAL PRAYERS

—10—

SALVATION

Father, Your Word says You loved me so much that You sent Your very own Son, Jesus, to die for my sin so I could live with You forever. I know that I am a sinner. I say out loud with my mouth that Jesus is my Lord, and I believe in my heart that You, God, raised Him from the dead.

I accept Your forgiveness and cleansing from all my sin. I receive the free gift of eternal life right now. I invite You to come into my heart and life. I want to trust Jesus as Savior and follow Him as Lord.

In Jesus' name I pray. Amen.

SCRIPTURE REFERENCES

Psalm 103:12	Romans 10:9,10,13
John 3:16	Ephesians 2:8,9
Romans 3:23	1 John 1:9
Romans 6:23	

—11—

CONFESSION:
"I AM GOD'S CHILD"

Behold what manner of love the Father has bestowed upon me, that I should be called a son/daughter of God; therefore the world knows me not, because it knew Him not.

Thank You for choosing me — for appointing me — that I might go and bear fruit and keep on bearing; that my fruit may be lasting. I have received and welcomed Jesus and stand in the power and authority to become a child of God.

Father, I am led by Your Spirit; therefore I am Your child. I have not received the spirit of bondage again to fear; but I have received the Spirit of adoption, whereby I cry Abba, Father. The Spirit itself bears witness with my spirit, that I am a child of God. And since I am Your child, I am an heir: an heir of God, and a joint-heir with Christ.

Father, I will not be unequally yoked together with unbelievers, for I am the temple of the living God. You dwell in me and walk in me; You are my God, and I am Your child. I come out from among the world, and I will be separate. I will not touch the unclean thing; therefore You receive me as Your child.

I rejoice, Father, because You have said, ...**I will receive you, and will be a Father unto you, and ye shall be my sons and daughters...** (2 Cor. 6:16,17 KJV). You are the Lord Almighty, and there has not failed one word of all Your good promise.

Today I am a child of God,
A God Who sees, a God Who hears,
A God Who watches over me.
Today I am a child of God.

SCRIPTURE REFERENCES

1 Kings 8:56 KJV   John 17:11,16 KJV

John 1:12 AMP   2 Corinthians 6:14-18

KJV

John 15:16 AMP   1 John 3:1 KJV

—12—

INFILLING OF THE HOLY SPIRIT

Father, I thank You that You have made it possible for me to be empowered in my Christian walk. You have sent the Holy Spirit as a Comforter, so that I can have power to witness and live a successful life.

I have received Your salvation through Jesus Christ. I am Your child; therefore, I am qualified to receive the Holy Spirit because I know Jesus as my Lord and Savior.

I understand that although the Holy Spirit gives me the words and phrases, I am responsible for speaking and allowing the Holy Spirit to give me my heavenly prayer language.

Father, when I speak in my heavenly prayer language, I am not speaking to men, but to You. Even though my mind does not understand what I am saying, my spirit does — and so do You. I know that I can pray with my prayer language as an act of my will. I thank You that praying in the Holy Spirit strengthens me and encourages my faith in You, and that I can pray mysteries in the Holy Ghost concerning my life and Your plan for me. I can pray with my spirit, and I can pray with my understanding.

Your Word says that, as our heavenly Father, You give the Holy Spirit to those who ask. I ask You for the gift of the Holy Spirit. I receive Him now by faith. Thank You for filling me with the power of the Holy Ghost. I will yield myself to Him and begin to speak with other tongues.

In Jesus' name I pray. Amen.

SCRIPTURE REFERENCES

Luke 11:9-13   1 Corinthians 14:2,14,15

John 14:16,17   1 John 5:14,15

Acts 1:8   Jude 20

Acts 2:4,38

—13—

FAVOR WITH PARENTS, TEACHERS, FRIENDS, CO-WORKERS, OR EMPLOYERS

Father, I ask for favor with You and with all men. I will keep Your laws and obey Your commands. I will remember to be truthful and kind from deep within my heart, then I will find favor with both You and man. I will acquire a reputation for good judgment and common sense.

Father, in the name of Jesus, You make Your face to shine upon and enlighten me and are gracious (kind, merciful, and giving favor) to me. I am the head and not the tail. I am above only and not beneath.

Because I seek Your Kingdom, and Your righteousness, and diligently seek good, I produce favor. I am a blessing to You, Lord, and a blessing to _____ *(name them: family, neighbors, business associates, school mates, friends, teachers etc.)*. Grace (favor) is with me because I love the Lord Jesus in sincerity. I extend favor, honor, and love to _____ *(names)*. I am flowing in Your love, Father. You are pouring out upon me the spirit of favor. You crown me with glory and honor for I am Your child — Your workmanship.

I am a success today. I am someone very special to You, Lord. I am growing in the Lord — waxing strong in spirit.

Father, You give me knowledge and skill in all learning and wisdom.

You bring me to find favor, compassion, and loving-kindness with _____ *(names)*. I obtain favor in the sight of all who look upon me this day, in the name of Jesus. I am filled with Your fullness — rooted and grounded in love. You are doing exceeding abundantly above all that I ask or think for Your mighty power is taking over in me.

Thank You, Father, that I am well-favored by You and by man.

In Jesus' name I pray. Amen.

SCRIPTURE REFERENCES

Numbers 6:25 AMP   Zechariah 12:10 AMP

Deuteronomy 28:13 AMP   Matthew 6:33 AMP

Esther 2:15,17 KJV   Luke 2:40 KJV

Psalm 8:5 AMP   Luke 6:38 AMP

Proverbs 3:1-4 TLB   Ephesians 2:10 AMP

Proverbs 11:27 AMP   Ephesians 3:19,20 KJV

Daniel 1:17,9 AMP   Ephesians 6:24 AMP

—14—

YOUR APPEARANCE

Father, I thank You for making me and for giving me life. Your Word says that You created me in Your likeness and in Your image. I thank You that You created me good. You knit me together in my mother's womb. My frame was not hidden from You when I was being formed in secret [and] intricately and curiously wrought [as if embroidered with various colors]. I know that Jesus came so that I could enjoy life to its fullest.

I speak Your Words of life to myself. I will spend time developing a quiet and meek spirit. I know that my outward appearance is also important to You for You care about every area of my life. You give me the desires of my heart when I delight myself in You and commit my ways to You. I desire to feel good about myself, so that I will be confident and present myself well.

Help me to learn how to take care of myself, and to maximize all the natural gifts that You gave me when You created me. Help me to listen to the Holy Spirit, the Teacher on the inside of me, keeping in mind that my body is His temple. I will control and discipline my body. I believe that with Your help, I can lose weight, or add and tone muscles to maximize the physical beauty of the body that You gave me.

Father, help me to exercise consistently and to take care of this temple of the Holy Spirit. Help me to be patient and to change any lifestyle or eating habits that might be destructive. Your Word is life to me and health to all my flesh. I thank You for the beauty of a godly character. I treat my body with respect because Your Holy Spirit lives in me.

I am so valuable that You gave Your only Son for my salvation. I believe that You are still perfecting everything that involves me, including the way I look.

In Jesus' name I pray. Amen.

SCRIPTURE REFERENCES

Genesis 1:26,27,31	Isaiah 44:2
Psalm 37:4,5 KJV	John 3:16
Psalm 100:3 KJV	John 10:10
Psalm 138:8 KJV	1 Corinthians 6:19,20
Psalm 139:13,15 AMP	1 Corinthians 9:25-27 AMP
Psalm 149:4	1 Peter 3:4
Proverbs 4:20-22	1 Peter 5:7 KJV
Proverbs 31:30	

—15—

MEETING NEW FRIENDS

Father, I come boldly to Your throne to ask You to help me to meet some new friends. I know that You are the source of love and friendship, but You also desire to express Your love and friendship toward me through others. So, I am convinced that it is Your will for me to have godly friendships with members of both sexes.

Your Word reveals the purpose and value of healthy friendships. It is not the quantity, but the quality of friends that matters.

Holy Spirit, teach me what I need to know to be a quality friend. Help me to show myself friendly to others and to love my friends at all times.

I purpose to live in peace as much as is possible, and pray that when my friends and I come together we will encourage each other. Help me to rid myself of any prejudice or partiality. I will not [attempt to] hold [and] practice the faith of our Lord Jesus Christ [the Lord] of glory [together with snobbery]! I will welcome and receive others as You, Father, have received me.

Help me to be kind, humble, and gentle. Help me to forgive those who need forgiveness, because I am forgiven. For my new friends, I thank You.

In Jesus' name I pray. Amen.

SCRIPTURE REFERENCES

Psalm 84:11	Ephesians 4:2,32 AMP
Proverbs 13:20	Philippians 1:27
Proverbs 17:17	Philippians 2:2
Ecclesiastes 4:9,10	Colossians 2:2 KJV
John 15:13	Hebrews 4:16 KJV
Romans 15:7 AMP	James 1:17
1 Corinthians 1:10	James 2:1 AMP

—16—

SELF-ESTEEM

Father, I come to Your throne room in order to receive help for my self-image. You created me in Your image and likeness, and that means so much to me. I know that You always love me. I know You didn't just carelessly or thoughtlessly throw me together. You made me so wonderfully complex! It is amazing to think about. Your workmanship is marvelous — and how well I know it.

Because I am Your workmanship, Your handicraft, made for good works, I ask You to help me to view myself from Your perspective. Help me to realize my strengths. Open my eyes to the strengths, abilities, and talents that You have placed inside of me. Give me grace to find the good that is in me. Help me to be appreciative of who I am, instead of critical of who I am not.

Although the world places importance on physical appearance, Father, I know that You judge men's hearts. You are interested in a pure heart and a humble spirit. I know that I am very valuable to You. Knowing that I am chosen makes me feel special. Thank You for choosing me before the foundation of the world. I acknowledge You, God, as my Father, and thank You that I am Your child.

Help me to set my affections on things above rather than on things of the world. Help me to mature in my relationship with You and to develop into the happy, joyful, strong Christian that I have the potential to be.

In Jesus' name I pray. Amen.

SCRIPTURE REFERENCES

Genesis 1:27   Ephesians 2:10 AMP

1 Samuel 16:7   Colossians 3:2 KJV

Psalm 139:14   Hebrews 4:16 KJV

Isaiah 57:15 KJV   1 Peter 2:9

Romans 12:1   1 Peter 4:10

2 Corinthians 6:18   1 John 3:1-3

Ephesians 1:4

—17—

BOLDNESS

Father, help me to be bolder. Help me not to confuse boldness with being loud, obnoxious, or rude, but to recognize that true boldness comes from knowing that I know that I abide in Jesus and that Jesus and His Word abide in me. Boldness comes not by might nor by power, but by Your Spirit.

Father, I want to be bold with my love just as Jesus was bold with His love. I desire a quiet confidence and assurance that comes from knowing You. Please give me the wisdom to know when to be quiet and when to speak out. Open my eyes so that I can see people as Jesus sees them. Thank You for giving me a heart of compassion and love for everyone.

I am not ashamed of You, Father, and I am not ashamed of the Gospel of Jesus Christ. Because I really love people, I am not afraid to tell them about Jesus.

Thank You for giving me the words to say, so that when I talk to others, it is like You, God, talking to them. I will live in an exemplary manner representing You by both my words and my actions. My behavior will reflect love, joy, and peace to others.

I thank You that I am not hindered by fear, because You have not given me a spirit of fear, but of power and of love and of a sound mind. I know that perfect love casts out all fear. So by faith, I believe that I will not be intimidated by what other people think or say or do.

Thank You for courage and strength to love and to live like Jesus. I am asking You for boldness, wisdom, and freedom to declare Your message fearlessly at just the right time to my friends at school and at work.

In Jesus' name I pray. Amen.

SCRIPTURE REFERENCES

Proverbs 28:1	2 Corinthians 4:4-6
Zechariah 4:6	Ephesians 6:19
Matthew 10:19,20 KJV	2 Timothy 1:7 KJV
Mark 16:15,16	Hebrews 13:6 KJV
John 15:7,8 KJV	James 1:5
Acts 4:13,29,33	1 Peter 4:11
Romans 1:16	1 John 4:18 KJV
Romans 5:5	

—18—

BEFORE A DATE*

Father, Your Word says that Jesus came that I might enjoy life to the fullest. So I thank You for the friends You have given me to date. Please teach me how to be a friend as Jesus would be. I want to bring out the very best in others, and to help them have fun and enjoy life.

Thank You for giving me different and creative ideas for things to do on a date that are fun and exciting for us and pleasing to You. Help us not to be nervous, but just to be ourselves.

Father, I thank You that my date and I don't have to be phony or try to be someone else. We can let our own personalities show because we are both made in Your image, with fun and interesting personalities.

---

* Because the Word of God instructs that children should honor and respect their parents, dating — especially among younger teens — should be with parents' permission. See Ephesians 6:1-3.

I realize that I can be a positive or a negative influence on others, but I choose to be a good influence for You. I commit this relationship to You. I thank You that You have given me good judgment so that I will not form improper relationships. I will be respectful of our parents, and be sure to get home on time. I will practice good manners and conduct myself like a gentleman/lady. I will avoid the very appearance of evil. I will keep my body holy. I trust You for the wisdom I need in every area of my life so that I react properly to every situation.

Thank You for Your protection as we go out, because Your angels are assigned to us so we will not get hurt. I know that You hear me when I pray, so I expect to have a good date, a date filled with fun, joy, laughter, excitement, and peace. I believe that we will have an evening full of good conversation, and I thank You that I will have the right words to say at the end of the date.

Father, thank You for helping me to look and act my very best.

In Jesus' name I pray. Amen.

SCRIPTURE REFERENCES

Genesis 1:27	Ephesians 4:29
Psalm 91:11,12	Ephesians 6:1-3
Proverbs 3:1-4 TLB	Colossians 4:6
John 10:10	1 Thessalonians 5:22 KJV
John 13:34,35	2 Timothy 1:7 KJV
Romans 12:1	Hebrews 10:24
1 Corinthians 5:9-11	James 1:5
2 Corinthians 6:14-18	1 John 5:14,15

—19—

BEFORE AN EXAM

Father, thank You for Your Word that says You've given me a spirit of love, of power, and of a sound mind. Not a defective, handicapped, weak or sickly mind, but one full of strength, vitality, and soundness. You have said that I have the mind of Christ. It is written that Jesus grew in wisdom, stature, and favor with God and man.

I believe I have the capacity to learn and to make excellent grades. In Daniel's life, You caused him to be ten times greater in knowledge than the men of the world. I believe that as I exercise faith in Your Word, the mind of Christ will be working in my life.

As I prepare for this exam, show me what to study and how to study most effectively. May the Holy Spirit cause me to be of quick understanding. Help me to develop the powers of concentration, so I can maximize the ability You have given me. Help me to discipline my mind to think on the subject matter at hand, and not daydream and lazily wander around, so I can get the most from my study time.

Father, as I enter to take this exam, I ask You to help me. Grant me wisdom and show me how to take the test, so that I gain the most points and make the best grade I can make, using the knowledge that I have to the best of my ability.

Help me to stay full of peace. I cast down those thoughts of fear and helplessness, and replace them with thoughts of faith and wisdom.

In Jesus' name I pray. Amen.

SCRIPTURE REFERENCES

Daniel 1:17,20	Galatians 6:9
Luke 2:52	Ephesians 3:20

John 14:26,27   Philippians 2:13

Romans 8:37   Philippians 4:13

1 Corinthians 2:16   Colossians 3:15,23,24

2 Corinthians 3:5   2 Timothy 1:7

2 Corinthians 10:5 KJV   James 1:5

—20—

BEFORE A SPECIAL SCHOOL EVENT

Father, I am glad that You care about every area of my life. I am asking You for the wisdom and strength to be the best that I can be in this event.

I don't have to worry about anything because You have not given me a spirit of fear, but of power, of love, and of a sound mind. Because Your Word says that perfect love casts out all fear, I give every worry or concern to You. I know that You always give me grace to help me when I need it. Help me to act like Jesus in everything I do and especially in this event.

I pray for all those who are performing with me. I want people to know I am a Christian because I act like one. I realize that everything I do is a reflection of You. You give me the talents, abilities, and confidence to be successful in all that I do. Because I am doing all things for You, and not to impress other people, I do them with all my heart and strength.

Thank You for helping me to develop my abilities so that I can do well. Please help me to keep a good attitude during every event. I won't let strife, hatred, or any wrong thinking enter into my mind.

Thank You, Father, for helping me to control my tongue so that everything I say and do will be a light to those people I come in contact with. Help me to handle both success and failure with poise and grace.

Lord, thank You that You made me for fellowship and friendship with You and with others; and thank You for filling my life with events that help me to learn, to grow, and to achieve.

In Jesus' name I pray. Amen.

SCRIPTURE REFERENCES

Exodus 15:2	2 Timothy 1:7 KJV
Ecclesiastes 9:10 KJV	Hebrews 4:16
Isaiah 41:10	James 1:5,6
John 13:34,35	James 3:2
2 Corinthians 10:5	1 Peter 4:11
Philippians 4:6	1 Peter 5:7 KJV
Colossians 3:23	1 John 4:18 KJV

—21—

BEFORE A VACATION
OR A ROAD TRIP*

Father, I set my expectations and hopes upon You because You generously provide me with everything for my enjoyment. I look to You to fill me with Your joy and peace as we have fun, excitement, laughter, and adventure on this vacation/road trip. I cast all my cares upon You right now. I refuse to worry or fret about anything.

Please lead and guide me, and speak to my heart during this time away. Help me to meet and to make new friends while we travel. Make me a blessing to others and use me as a witness to those I meet who don't know You. Grant me words of life to speak to their hearts so they can be born again.

---

*Because the Word of God instructs that children should honor and respect their parents, trips should be taken only with parents' permission — especially with younger teens.

See Ephesians 6:1-3.

As I travel, grant me eyes to see, ears to hear, and a heart to appreciate all of Your wonderful creation. Please show me those secret things that You share only with those who fear and respect You.

Thank You for granting me wisdom to handle every situation. Help me to travel intelligently and to act in a manner that is pleasing to You.

Thank You for giving Your angels charge over me to keep me in all my ways. They will bear me up in their hands and encamp all around me to protect me from all harm or evil. Thank You that You protect not only my physical body, but also all of my property. Thank You, Father, that the transportation vehicle will be safe and operate perfectly without problems.

I will be sure to spend time in Your Word and in prayer while I am away, and to go to church if the opportunity arises. I thank You that we will have excellent weather, and that this will be a fun, safe, exciting, and adventurous vacation/road trip filled with laughter,

rest, and relaxation — so that I can return refreshed
and rejuvenated.

In Jesus' name I pray. Amen.

SCRIPTURE REFERENCES

Psalm 23:2,3 AMP	Acts 3:19 AMP
Psalm 25:14	Romans 15:13
Psalm 34:7	Philippians 4:6,7
Psalm 91:10-12 KJV	1 Timothy 6:17
Psalm 127:2	James 3:5 KJV
Isaiah 54:17	1 Peter 5:7 KJV
Matthew 11:28	

—22—

BEFORE A SPORTS EVENT

Father, I thank You that You care about all the details of my life, even this sports event. Your Word says that I am strong and can do all things because I have Jesus in my heart. I believe that You will guide my performance.

I have practiced diligently, and You have said that the hand of the diligent shall rule. I will run this race and play this game in such a way that I might win. In Philippians 3:14 (KJV) the Apostle Paul said, **I press toward the mark for the prize of the high calling of God....** In like manner I strive to win, to do my best, and to compete according to the rules in integrity and purity of heart. I will compete with all my strength and might, because I play for Your glory.

Father, I ask You for wisdom, for Your Word says that wisdom is better than strength. Help me to compete skillfully and confidently. I believe I have the mind of Christ. Though others may look to their superior abilities, or their wealth of experience, I look to and trust in You.

I pray for my teammates. I ask that You help us play together as a team, that each one of us will contribute our individual strengths and cover one another's weaknesses. Grant our coach wisdom to make the right call at the right time. Help him/her coach effectively, inspiring us to play harder, edifying us, and building character in us.

Father, build in me the character of a godly competitor — that under pressure I may walk in peace, maintaining poise. When I am tempted to become discouraged and give up, I will continue, empowered by Your strength. When faced with overwhelming odds, I will not waver in unbelief, but will walk securely because I know that nothing is impossible with You.

I will not murmur, complain, gossip, or get offended at the officials, coaches, opposing team, or at my own team if something happens that I don't like.

When graced with victory, I will not become prideful, because pride goes before a fall, but will gratefully give You all the glory. If we should lose, I will resist the temptation to become discouraged, because I know that You always cause us to triumph in Christ Jesus, and that we are always winners through Him.

Father, thank You that both teams can play free from injury. I pray that this will be a fair game and a just game. Thank You that the officials will be fair and impartial and will keep all things decent and in order.

Thank You that I can do all things through Christ Who strengthens me. No matter what the results of this game, I will exercise the fruit of the Spirit and be a gracious athlete.

In Jesus' name I pray. Amen.

SCRIPTURE REFERENCES

Psalm 91:11,12	Romans 4:20
Proverbs 4:12	1 Corinthians 2:16
Proverbs 12:24 KJV	1 Corinthians 10:31
Proverbs 16:18	2 Corinthians 2:14 KJV
Ecclesiastes 9:10,16	Galatians 5:22,23
Isaiah 40:31	Philippians 4:13
Joel 3:10 KJV	Colossians 3:23
Luke 1:37	James 1:5
John 6:43 KJV	1 Peter 5:7 KJV

—23—

PART-TIME OR FULL-TIME JOB*

Father, thank You that You are my Provider and my Source of total supply. Every good thing that I have comes from You. I believe You will show me a way to earn money.

I ask in the name of Jesus for a job that pays enough to meet all of my financial needs. Your Word says that it is good for me to enjoy the results of my labor. It is a gift from You that I am happy where I work. It is my goal to do my best on my job so that I will gain the respect and favor of my co-workers and my employers.

---

* Because the Word of God instructs that children should honor their parents, having a part-time or full-time job should be with parents' permission — especially with younger teens. See Ephesians 6:1-3.

Help me not to grow tired of doing what is right. Teach me the best way to manage my money so that I won't waste it or throw it away.

I thank You, Father, that You are leading me to the best possible job. Thank You for a job that will not conflict with my relationship with You, or with any of my family, school, or church priorities.

Help me to develop a strong work ethic and to have an excellent and enthusiastic attitude.

Help me to be obedient to my employer. If something goes against my conscience, help me to be bold and clear in my communication to the people who can change things so that it won't make a bad scene.

Help me to be an effective witness for the Gospel. I will work hard, diligently, and quietly with a humble spirit at all times, not just when my boss is around, but as if I were working for You, because I am working for You.

Thank You that I am strong because of You, Father. I will not give up, but I trust that my work will be recognized and rewarded. Thank You for Your protection so I don't have to be nervous or afraid of anything, but I share my requests with You in prayer. Thanks for Your peace that protects my heart and mind in every situation.

Father, please help me to have absolute and complete control over my tongue, what I say, so that I won't hurt or offend anyone. I won't murmur, complain, backbite, or gossip.

Thank You that I have favor with my boss and with all of the people I work with.

In Jesus' name I pray. Amen.

SCRIPTURE REFERENCES

Deuteronomy 8:18   Ephesians 6:5-7

2 Chronicles 15:7   Philippians 4:6,7,19

Proverbs 11:27 AMP	Colossians 3:23,24
Ecclesiastes 5:18-20	1 Thessalonians 4:11,12
Isaiah 48:17 KJV	2 Thessalonians 3:13
John 6:43 KJV	James 1:5,17
1 Corinthians 15:58	James 3:2

—24—

YOUR FUTURE

Father, I am dedicated to live for You. I don't know everything the future holds for me, but I know that it is in Your hands. I trust You to lead me, to be my guide in life. I trust You to prepare me now for Your life plan for me. Thank You for the wisdom to discern the right timing for what You would have me do in each season of my life. I choose to love, obey, and cleave unto You with my whole body, soul, and spirit.

If college is in my future, please help me to select the right one. Thank You for providing the means for me to go. If it is not college, then prepare me for my job. Help me to recognize the skills You have given me so that I can develop them and give the glory to You. Give me understanding and light so that I am quick to learn. I thank You for the wisdom and light that come from You and Your Word.

You are a help to me in everything I do. If it is Your will for me to marry someday, I thank You that You are not only preparing me, but that You are also working on my future spouse. Until that time comes, help me to be content in every situation.

I believe that You will supply all the money I need to do Your will. I believe You will instruct me and teach me which way to go. You don't make things confusing for me, but You make a clear path for me when I put You first.

Thank You for Your words which are a light for my path and for Your Holy Spirit Who reveals to me Your plan for me. I treasure my life with and for You. Thank You, Father, for holding me and my future in the palm of Your hand.

In Jesus' name I pray. Amen.

SCRIPTURE REFERENCES

Deuteronomy 30:20	John 16:13
Psalm 25:5	Romans 8:14
Psalm 32:8	1 Corinthians 2:9,10
Psalm 119:105	Ephesians 1:16-18
Proverbs 3:5,6	Ephesians 2:10
Proverbs 4:18	Philippians 4:11,13,19
Ecclesiastes 3:1-8	Hebrews 13:5
Isaiah 49:16	1 Peter 5:7
Jeremiah 33:3	

— 25 —

DEDICATION OF YOUR TITHES

I profess this day unto the Lord God that I have come into the inheritance which the Lord swore to give me. I am in the land which You have provided for me in Jesus Christ, the Kingdom of Almighty God. I was a sinner serving Satan; he was my god. But I called upon the name of Jesus, and You heard my cry and delivered me into the Kingdom of Your dear Son.

Jesus, as my Lord and High Priest, I bring the first-fruits of my income to You and worship the Lord my God with it.

I rejoice in all the good which You have given to me and my household. I have hearkened to the voice of the Lord my God and have done according to all that You have commanded me. Now look down from Your holy habitation from heaven and bless me as You said in Your Word. I thank You, Father, in Jesus' name. Amen.

SCRIPTURE REFERENCES

Deuteronomy 26:1,3, 10,11,14,15 AMP

Colossians 1:13

Hebrews 3:1,7,8

Ephesians 2:1-5

—26—

PEACEFUL SLEEP

Father, thank You for peaceful sleep, and for Your angels that encamp around us who fear You. You deliver us and keep us safe. The angels excel in strength, do Your Word, and heed the voice of Your Word. You give Your angels charge over me, to keep me in all my ways.

I bring every thought, every imagination, and every dream into the captivity and obedience of Jesus Christ. Father, I thank You that, even as I sleep, my heart counsels me and reveals to me Your purpose and plan. Thank You for sweet sleep, for You promised Your beloved sweet sleep. Therefore, my heart is glad and my spirit rejoices. My body and soul rest and confidently dwell in safety. Amen.

SCRIPTURE REFERENCES

Proverbs 3:24   Psalm 91:11

Psalm 34:7   2 Corinthians 10:5

Psalm 103:20

Part III

PRAYERS FOR OTHERS

—27—

PARENTS AND FAMILY

Father, I bring my parents and family before You in prayer. Thank You that we have been blessed with all spiritual blessings in Christ Jesus. Your Word says that it takes wisdom to build a good family and understanding to make it strong. I ask that You make my parents strong and wise. Please fill them with the knowledge that they need in order to build a strong, healthy relationship together.

Help Dad to act and speak in love toward Mom. Help them to submit one to the other under the loving leadership of Dad. Help them to communicate with one another and to pray with each other that their relationship may thrive, so they can be more in love now than they were when they were first married.

I pray that my brothers, sisters, and I will obey, honor, and respect our parents' authority, that we may live in peace and quiet so that things will go well with us and we will live a long life on this earth. I pray that my family is founded and securely built upon Your Word, like the house that was founded upon the rock and built so securely that when the flood came, the house couldn't be shaken.

Help Dad to be the spiritual leader of our household, and grant him the wisdom he needs to raise us with faith, encouragement, and love. Please give Dad and Mom the insight to know when and how to discipline us so that we turn out right. Help Dad to guide our family so that he may boldly proclaim, "As for me and my house, we will serve the Lord."

Help us to bear with each other and forgive each other, as You have forgiven us, and to love each other as You have loved us. I want the peace of God to rule in our hearts. Open our eyes that we may realize the gift of God that is in each one of us, so that we no longer view one another from a human point of view, but from Your point of view. Help us to value, respect, and be grateful for each other, instead of taking each other for granted. Help us to remember that because we are members of one body, we are called to work together peacefully.

Father, I pray that my parents and family and I will always choose to serve You, and that our hearts will forever be knit together in love. I pray that our home will be a place of safety and refuge, a place of encouragement, filled with laughter, happiness, love, and joy.

Thank You so much for providing for all of our physical, emotional, and financial needs. Thank You for giving Your angels charge over us so that our home is safe from all danger, harm, or evil.

In Jesus' name I pray. Amen.

SCRIPTURE REFERENCES

Joshua 24:15 KJV   Ephesians 4:25

Psalm 91:11   Ephesians 5:21,22,25

Psalm 112:1,3   Ephesians 6:1-3 AMP

Proverbs 24:3 EB   Philippians 2:2

Luke 6:48   Philippians 4:19

John 15:12   Colossians 2:2 KJV

2 Corinthians 5:16 AMP   Colossians 3:13-15

Ephesians 1:3 KJV   1 Timothy 2:2

—28—

BOYFRIEND/GIRLFRIEND*

Father, I know that You care about every area of my life, especially who I date. So I believe that _____ is blessed with all spiritual blessings in Christ Jesus. Thank You that he/she is a friend I can grow with, learn from, and have fun with.

I know that as we put You first and keep our relationship with You close through Your Word and prayer, You will bless this relationship. Help us to communicate with each other so we will have an understanding of the differences between the way men and women think and see things.

---

* Because the Word of God instructs that children should honor and respect their parents, dating — especially with younger teens — should be with parents' permission. See Ephesians 6:1-3.

Thank You for bringing _____ into my life so we can encourage each other to grow closer to You, Father. Help me to be a blessing to him/her so that I can contribute something valuable into his/her life. Thank You that he/she will like me for who I am, and love You because of Who You are. I pray that _____ will stay on fire for You and love Jesus more and more, so that we can grow closer to You and minister to other people.

I know that unruly friends corrupt and destroy good morals. Help _____ to say no to these friends and to have You as his/her first love. You comfort him/her when no one else can. Help him/her to be content in his/her relationship with You. You are his/her friend when everyone else leaves. I thank You for the Holy Spirit Who will warn him/her of bad situations and lead him/her into good situations. Help us not to compromise our relationship with You.

Father, help _____ to be a doer of the Word. Help us to treat each other with purity in our relationship. Help us to keep our relationship in perspective; we are brother and sister in the Lord, and help us to act accordingly. I pray that our relationship will be a healthy one, bringing growth and maturity to both of our lives. And thank You that _____ has favor and a good relationship with my family, because I know that this is important to You. Help us just to relax and develop our friendship.

Father, I pray that we will always listen to Your Voice and that we will always be sensitive to Your Spirit so that we don't set ourselves up for a fall. Help each of us to establish sexual, physical, emotional, and intellectual boundaries so we may walk, live, and conduct ourselves in a manner worthy of You. Thank You for Your angels who are protecting us from all harm, evil, or danger. Thank You for what You are doing in our lives.

In Jesus' name I pray. Amen.

SCRIPTURE REFERENCES

Psalm 37:4	1 Corinthians 15:33 AMP
Psalm 91:11	Ephesians 1:3 KJV
John 14:18	James 1:5,22 KJV
Romans 8:14	1 Peter 5:7

—29—

FUTURE SPOUSE

Father, I seek first Your Kingdom and Your righteousness, and all things shall be mine as well. I know that You love me and that I can trust Your Word: For in Him the whole fullness of Deity (the Godhead) continues to dwell in bodily form — giving complete expression of the divine nature. And I am in Him, made full and have come to the fullness of life — in Christ I too am filled with the Godhead: Father, Son, and Holy Spirit, and reach full spiritual stature. And Christ is the Head of all rule and authority — of every angelic principality and power. Because of Jesus, I am complete; He is my Lord.

I come before You, Father, desiring a Christian mate. I petition that Your will be done in my life, and I enter into that blessed rest by adhering to, trusting in, and relying on You.

Father, You desire that I live a life free from care, that I should be content and satisfied in every situation that I am in, and that I should not be anxious or worried about anything. You have said that if I am willing and obedient to Your Word, You will give me the desires of my heart. It is my desire that someday I will be married to the person You have chosen for me.

I pray for him/her. Father, especially help him/her to grow in love, Your kind of love. A friend loves at all times, and I desire for my spouse to be my very best friend. I desire that my spouse be a person who shares the same love that I have for You, someone who will be one in spirit and purpose with me.

I ask You to send mature men and women into our lives to give us good, godly counsel and to teach us how we should love each other and care for our family. Teach us both what You expect husbands and wives to do and how we ought to behave toward each other. Reveal to our hearts Your Word concerning the marriage relationship and correct any wrong thinking in our lives. Grant us knowledge through godly people, books, tapes, and preaching that will give us understanding concerning relationships, so that we can avoid damaging the relationship You desire for us.

Father, I trust You to lead me and guide me by Your Holy Spirit so that when Your perfect time is right, I will have the wisdom, discretion, and discernment to know that my choice and Yours are the same for my life-mate. I am secure with the mind and the spirit that You have given me to make this decision.

I pray that the eyes of my future spouse's understanding will be opened so that he/she will have complete knowledge of Your will in all spiritual wisdom and understanding. I pray that he/she will live a life that is worthy of You, Lord, and pleasing to You in every way. Thank You that he/she will always be involved in doing good deeds, and have a strong, growing relationship with You. I pray that our commitment to each other will continually grow as we draw closer to You.

In Jesus' name I pray. Amen.

SCRIPTURE REFERENCES

Genesis 2:18-24	Ephesians 5:22-25
Psalm 37:4,5 KJV	Philippians 2:2-7
Psalm 130:5	Philippians 4:6,11 AMP
Proverbs 17:17 KJV	Colossians 1:9,10
Isaiah 1:19 KJV	Colossians 2:9,10 AMP
Matthew 6:33 RSV	Hebrews 4:3,10 AMP

—30—

FRIENDS AND CLASSMATES

Father, I thank You for all of my friends and class-mates. I believe that You are able to do exceeding abun-dantly above all that I ask or think, so I am believing for some outstanding relationships in my life.

I pray for the friends You have already blessed me with. Help us to be faithful in our relationships with each other, and to be trustworthy with the secrets we share. Help us to be loving toward each other at all times, even when we may disappoint each other. Help us to challenge each other in our walk with You so that we develop in character and sharpen each other as iron sharpens iron. Grant us times of heart-to-heart talks and times when we can encourage one another. Help us to love each other as You have loved us, and to be sen-sitive to one another, laying down our own lives and being unselfish by taking the time to pray for each other. May our hearts be strengthened as they are knit together in Your love.

Father, please help my friends to live their lives as You want them to so that they will always please You. Open the eyes of their understanding that the spirit of wisdom and revelation will be upon them so they can see that You are able to do exceeding abundantly above all that they ask or think. I ask You to bless them and touch everything they do so that it is successful and prosperous. Thank You for helping them to have great family relationships. Help them to find favor with You, with their teachers, and with all other people.

I thank You that they can see the light of Jesus and the salvation that He brings. Thank You for giving them undeserved favor and spiritual strength and a better understanding of Your Word. I believe that Your angels will watch over and protect them from any harm or evil in the world. Thank You for providing for their every financial need and helping them to always triumph in Jesus.

In Jesus' name I pray. Amen.

SCRIPTURE REFERENCES

Psalm 91:10,11,16	Ephesians 1:17,18 KJV
Proverbs 3:4,7	Ephesians 3:20 KJV
Proverbs 17:17 KJV	Philippians 1:9-11
Proverbs 27:5,6,9,17	Philippians 4:19
John 1:8,9	Colossians 2:2 KJV
John 3:16	James 5:16
John 12:32	2 Peter 3:18 AMP
John 15:13 KJV	1 John 3:24
2 Corinthians 2:14	1 John 4:9-12
2 Corinthians 4:4	

—31—

UNBELIEVERS AT SCHOOL

I am asking You, Father, to send forth laborers, including me, into my school. Cause us to be bold and filled with the Spirit, that we may be fearless in speech, and behave in such a way that we do all things pleasing in Your sight. Help my life to be a positive testimony for You to use. I am asking You for the outpouring of the Holy Spirit at my school, that the manifestations of the Holy Spirit will be in operation, to turn people's attention toward You.

I thank You for revival in the hearts of every Christian at my school, Lord. I pray that there will be a love for You, for prayer, and for Your Word — a new love for the things of God and a new love for souls — so that Christians won't just sit around, but will begin to share Your love with those who are lost.

Father, Your Word says that supernatural signs will follow those who believe in Jesus' name. I believe that these signs will follow us wherever we go.

I ask that the blinders will be removed from the eyes of the people at my school. I pray specifically for _____. I ask You to give me an anointing that I will know how to speak a timely word to him/her. Send me with Your Word to open his/her eyes and to help turn him/her from darkness to light and from the power of Satan to the power of God, so that he/she may receive forgiveness of sins, and make Jesus his/her Lord.

Father, I ask You to give me the sinners at my school as my inheritance. Use the perfect laborer to get them born again and filled with the Spirit.

Thank You for working in the lives of the people for whom I am praying. Thank You for revival at my school.

In Jesus' name I pray. Amen.

Every day after praying this prayer, thank the Lord for the salvation of your schoolmates. Rejoice and praise God for the victory! Confess the above prayer as done! Thank God for sending the laborers. Thank Him that Satan is bound. Alleluia!

SCRIPTURE REFERENCES

Job 22:30	Acts 26:17,18
Psalm 2:8	Romans 10:14
Proverbs 25:11 TLB	2 Corinthians 3:6
Proverbs 28:1	2 Corinthians 4:3,4
Isaiah 51:16	Ephesians 1:18
Matthew 9:37 KJV	1 John 5:14,15
Mark 16:15-18	

— 32 —

TEACHERS AT SCHOOL

Father, I thank You for my teachers. Please cause them to be a positive influence on the lives of their students. Help them to make learning fun, and to capture the attention of their classes in creative ways. I pray that they will be able to control the rebellious, calm the violent, motivate the lazy, direct the zealous, encourage the weak, and love the unloved.

I pray that if _____ is not born again, and does not have a personal relationship with Your Son Jesus, You will send someone to share Jesus with him/her and open his/her eyes to turn him/her from darkness to the light.

I pray that my teachers will skillfully develop the ability and knowledge You have given them. Instruct them and guide them in how and what they should teach so they can prepare us for what we will face when we graduate. I pray that they will have the respect for, and of, their students needed for the learning environment.

Father, I ask that You give my teachers insight and understanding into the lives of the students in their classes, so that they can help them with any problems they may be facing. I ask that You lead and guide my teachers into Your truth. I pray that You help them to have a strong relationship with You.

Thank You for encouraging them when they are upset and discouraged in their vocation. Help them to see the importance of their work in educating us. Give my teachers strength so they will not be tired of doing what is right. Help them to enjoy and experience the results of their persistence. Please bless them and their families, and prosper them financially so that they will have all their needs met. Protect them from any evil, danger, or injury.

Father, I pray that You will always guide my teachers to follow Your plan and uphold godliness in the classroom. Thank You that they have favor with their students and their parents, and with their administrators.

In Jesus' name I pray. Amen.

SCRIPTURE REFERENCES

Exodus 31:3,4 KJV	2 Corinthians 1:3,4
Psalm 32:8	2 Corinthians 3:5
Psalm 91:11	Galatians 6:9
Psalm 119:130	Ephesians 6:10,11
Proverbs 4:5-8	Philippians 2:13 KJV
Matthew 9:38	Philippians 4:19
John 16:13	Hebrews 6:10
Acts 26:17,18	

—33—

PASTOR AND YOUTH PASTOR

Father, You have said that You will give us shepherds according to Your heart, pastors who will feed us with knowledge and understanding. I thank You for my pastor and youth pastor. I receive and respect them as a gift from You. I ask You to give them a heart for the people in the congregation. Inspire and anoint them so they will feed us truth from Your Word.

You have said that the Good Shepherd gives His life for the sheep. Help them lay down their lives for us as we submit our lives to them. Teach them how to instruct and perfect us so that we can do the work of the ministry.

Father, give them a heart of compassion for those who are lost, that we may all effectively reach out to our community. Give them creativity to declare the

Gospel and to minister to the congregation in a way that is anointed and interesting.

Help their love to grow in knowledge and understanding of You so they can be completely sure of what is Your best. Grant my pastor and youth pastor a fresh anointing of Your wisdom, understanding, counsel, power, and knowledge. Give them times of rest and relaxation so they can be refreshed and rejuvenated.

Father, I ask that they may clearly share with others Your Son's salvation and bring Your healing to all those with broken hearts, and all who need healing. As they spend time with You, speak and reveal to them from Your Word truth that will set us free. Show them clearly and exactly what You would have them to do — how they are to guide the congregation. Show them Your plan and Your purpose and the goals that they should pursue.

Thank You for giving them freedom to speak, that they may boldly declare what You have placed in their hearts, that they may speak as the oracles of God, and be strengthened with Your anointing.

May they always walk in and teach Your love. Please help them to understand and guard the responsibility You have given them over our church and youth group. Help my pastor and youth pastor understand Your will in order to live a life worthy of the Gospel with purity and holiness. Protect them and their families by Your great power so that they will not be hurt.

Thank You for blessing my pastor, youth pastor, and our church financially so we can do what You have called us to do.

In Jesus' name I pray. Amen.

SCRIPTURE REFERENCES

Psalm 23:1-3   2 Corinthians 3:6

Isaiah 11:2,3   Ephesians 3:17-19

Jeremiah 3:15	Ephesians 4:11,15 KJV
Jeremiah 23:4	Ephesians 6:19
Jeremiah 29:11	Philippians 1:9
Matthew 9:36	Philippians 4:19
Matthew 11:28-30	Colossians 1:9-11
Luke 4:18	2 Timothy 1:13,14
John 8:31,32	1 Peter 4:11 KJV
John 10:11	1 Peter 5:2,3

—34—

LEADERS OF OUR COUNTRY

Father, thank You for the United States and its government. I pray for the president, the national and local government, the judges, the policemen, the business leaders, and all those who are in leadership positions in this country. Please protect them from the evil that is in the world and keep them safe and free from all harm.

Your Word says that when good men are in authority, the people celebrate, but when wicked men are in authority, the people are unhappy. I pray that You will keep good men and women in authority over my country. I ask that You promote and raise up a generation of able politicians who are men and women of truth, full of wisdom, and respectful towards You.

You have promised to bless any nation that follows after You. Help us to live quiet and peaceful lives so that we can continue to spread the Good News of the Gospel throughout the United States and the world.

I also pray that You give the men and women in leadership positions the understanding, wisdom, and ability to keep this country in order. I ask that You guide the president's heart and cause him to make decisions that will promote godliness. Please keep evil and wicked men from influencing the president. Keep his office based on things that are right.

Father, I pray for my brothers and sisters in the Lord who are in positions of leadership. I ask You to strengthen them in their hearts with all might by Your Spirit. Cause them to be bold and courageous. Surround them with favor as a shield, and expand their godly influence.

I pray for those in leadership positions who are not born again and who do not have a personal relationship with Your Son, Jesus. I pray that You will send someone to share Jesus with them and open their eyes to the light.

I pray for the Supreme Court. I ask that the men and women make righteous judgments, that they reach just and fair conclusions. Help the judges to inquire diligently, that they may make sound decisions. Turn their hearts to change past decisions and make new decisions that uphold goodness and godliness in our nation. If there is anyone who refuses godliness, I ask that he/she may be removed and replaced by one who respects godliness.

I ask that You cause the leaders of this country to make decisions that increase the integrity of our nation. Grant them the wisdom and insight needed to deal with this nation's finances, that You may cause us to prosper and be a blessing to other nations.

May Your Word multiply in our nation's capital so that our leaders may be better able to cooperate with Your plan and purpose.

Father, use this nation and its leaders in this great harvest of souls that will take place in the last days. I praise and thank You for blessing my country. I pray that our nation will accomplish the things that You want us to accomplish. I thank You that Jesus is Lord over the United States of America.

In Jesus' name I pray. Amen.

SCRIPTURE REFERENCES

1 Timothy 2:1-3	Matthew 13:39
Proverbs 29:2 KJV	Proverbs 25:5
Psalm 33:12	Proverbs 4:10-14
Proverbs 21:1	Proverbs 2:10-14,20,21
Proverbs 20:28	

—35—

COMFORT FOR A PERSON WHO HAS LOST A LOVED ONE

Father, in the name of Jesus I come boldly to Your throne of grace to obtain mercy and comfort for _____ in this time of need. I ask that the Holy Spirit comfort, soothe, and heal his/her broken heart.

Please give me the right words to say because I don't want to say anything that is trite or that will bring confusion. I only want to speak words that will minister life and peace to his/her heart. Help me to be quiet and say nothing if that is the best thing for me to do.

Father, I want to comfort those who need it, as You have comforted me. Help me to weep with those who weep. Your Word says that those who mourn are blessed by You, and will be comforted. Jesus was sent to heal the brokenhearted, so thank You for comforting and healing _____'s heart and letting him/her feel Your presence in a new and stronger way. Help him/her to be able to get on with his/her life after a normal grieving process.

In the name of Jesus, I bind any spirit of depression, guilt, or death that would try to attach itself to _____ and cause him/her to be paralyzed by grief and despair.

Thank You for lifting up _____ and giving him/her laughter for tears, and happiness and joy for sadness and mourning. Help him/her to look to You for comfort and to offer You praise for Your promise of renewed life.

If the loved one was a Christian, please help _____ to see that the departed is in heaven and in a much, much better place with You. And if _____ is not sure about where the loved one has gone, help him/her, Father, to make sure of his/her own salvation.

I pray now that if _____ is not born again, and does not have a personal relationship with Jesus, You will send someone to share Jesus with him/her and open his/her eyes to the light.

Finally, I ask that You help _____ to find Your peace and joy in this situation. I thank You that You are reassuring him/her that You are his/her strength. Show _____ that although people will leave, Jesus is a friend Who sticks closer than a brother, and that You will never leave nor forsake him/her.

I thank You, Father, for these things.

In Jesus' name I pray. Amen.

SCRIPTURE REFERENCES

Nehemiah 8:10	John 14:16,17
Psalm 119:50	Acts 26:17,18
Proverbs 18:24	Romans 12:15

Isaiah 61:1-3   2 Corinthians 1:3,4

Matthew 5:4   2 Corinthians 4:4

Matthew 18:18   Hebrews 4:15,16 AMP

Luke 4:18 KJV   Hebrews 13:5

—36—

DELIVERANCE OF A PERSON FROM A CULT

Father, in the name of Jesus, I come before You believing that Your Word runs swiftly throughout the earth. I bring _____ (all those and their families who are involved in cults) before You in prayer.

*In the name of Jesus I bind _____'s feet to the paths of righteousness that his/her steps would be steady and sure. I bind _____ to the work of the cross with all of its mercy, grace, love, forgiveness and dying to self.

I loose the power and effects of deceptions and lies from him/her. I loose the confusion and blindness of the god of this world from _____'s mind that have kept him/her from seeing the light of the gospel of Jesus Christ. I call forth every precious word of Scripture that has ever entered in his/her mind and heart that it would rise up in power within him/her. I loose the power and effects of any harsh or hard words (word curses) spoken to, about or by _____.

Execute justice, Father, for _____. Set the prisoners free, open the eyes of the blind, lift up the hurting, heal the brokenhearted, and bind up their wounds. Lift up the humble and needy, and turn back the hearts of the misled to obedience to Your will.

Father, You have told us in Your Word to restrain our voices from weeping and our eyes from tears, for our prayers will be rewarded. _____ will return from this cult and come again to his/her senses. Those who err in spirit will come to understanding.

I commission angels to go forth and dispel the forces of darkness and bring _____ home in the name of Jesus. I believe and say that _____ has had knowledge of and been acquainted with the Word which is able to instruct him/her and give him/her the understanding of the salvation which comes through faith in Christ Jesus. I pray and believe that You certainly will deliver and draw _____ to Yourself from every assault of evil, and that You will preserve and bring him/her safely into Your heavenly Kingdom.

In Jesus' name I pray. Amen.

Jesus gave me the keys and the authority to bind and loose these things in His name. Thank you, Lord, for the truth.

SCRIPTURE REFERENCES

Job 22:30	Jeremiah 31:16,17
Psalm 144:7,8 AMP	Jeremiah 46:27
Psalm 146:7,8 AMP	Luke 1:17 AMP
Psalm 147:3-6 AMP	2 Timothy 2:9
Psalm 147:15	2 Timothy 3:2-9,15
Isaiah 29:23,24 AMP	2 Timothy 4:18
Isaiah 43:5-7	Titus 1:11
Isaiah 49:25	Hebrews 1:14

* *Shattering Your Strongholds,* Copyright ©1992 by Liberty Savard, Bridge-Logos Publishers, North Brunswick, NJ (pp. 171-172)

Part IV

SPECIAL PRAYERS

— 37 —

VICTORY OVER FEAR

Father, when I am afraid, I will put my confidence in You. Yes, I will trust Your promises. And since I trust You, what can mere man do to me?

You have not given me a spirit of timidity, but of power and love and discipline (sound judgment). Therefore, I am not ashamed of the testimony of my Lord. I have not received a spirit of slavery leading to fear again, but I have received a spirit of adoption as a son, by which I cry out, "Abba! Father!"

Jesus, You delivered me, who, through fear of death, had been living all my life as a slave to constant dread. I receive the gift You left me — peace of mind and heart! And the peace You give isn't fragile like the peace the world gives. I cast away troubled thoughts, and I choose not to be afraid. I believe in God; I believe also in You.

Lord, You are my Light and my Salvation; You protect me from danger — whom shall I fear? When evil men come to destroy me, they will stumble and fall! Yes, though a mighty army marches against me, my heart shall know no fear! I am confident that You will save me.

Thank You, Holy Spirit, for bringing these things to my remembrance when I am tempted to be afraid. I will trust in my God. In the name of Jesus I pray. Amen.

SCRIPTURE REFERENCES

Psalm 56:3-5 TLB   Hebrews 2:15 TLB

2 Timothy 1:7,8 NAS   John 14:1,17 TLB

Romans 8:15 NAS   Psalm 27:1-3 TLB

—38—

VICTORY OVER PRIDE

Father, Your Word says that You hate a proud look, that You resist the proud but give grace to the humble. I submit myself, therefore, to You, God. In the name of Jesus, I resist the devil, and he will flee from me. I renounce every manifestation of pride in my life as sin; I repent and turn from it.

As an act of faith, I clothe myself with humility and receive Your grace. I humble myself under Your mighty hand, Lord, that You may exalt me in due time. I refuse to exalt myself. I do not think of myself more highly than I ought; I do not have an exaggerated opinion of my own importance, but rate my ability with sober judgment, according to the degree of faith apportioned to me.

Proverbs 11:2 says, "When pride cometh, then cometh shame: but with the lowly is wisdom." Father, I set myself to resist pride when it comes. My desire is to be counted among the lowly, so I take on the attitude of a servant.

Father, thank You that You dwell with one who is of a contrite and humble spirit. You revive the spirit of the humble and revive the heart of the contrite one. Thank You that the reward of humility and the reverent and worshipful fear of the Lord is riches and honor and life.

In Jesus' name I pray. Amen.

SCRIPTURE REFERENCES

Proverbs 6:16,17	Proverbs 11:2
James 4:6,7	Matthew 23:11
Proverbs 21:4	Isaiah 57:15
1 Peter 5:5,6	Proverbs 22:4 AMP
Romans 12:3 AMP	

—39—

OVERCOMING INTIMIDATION

Father, I come to You in the name of Jesus, confessing that intimidation has caused me to stumble. I ask Your forgiveness for thinking of myself as inferior, for I am created in Your image, and I am Your workmanship. Jesus said that the Kingdom of God is in me. Therefore, the power that raised Jesus from the dead dwells in me and causes me to face life with hope and divine energy.

The Lord is my Light and my Salvation; whom shall I fear? The Lord is the Strength of my life; of whom shall I be afraid? Lord, You said that You would never leave me or forsake me. Therefore, I can say without any doubt or fear that You are my Helper, and I am not afraid of anything that mere man can do to me. Greater is He that is in me than he that is in the world. If God is for me, who can be against me? I am free from the fear of man and public opinion.

Father, You have not given me a spirit of timidity — of cowardice, of craven and cringing and fawning fear — but You have given me a spirit of power and of love and of a calm and well-balanced mind and discipline and self-control. I can do all things through Christ Who gives me the strength. Amen.

SCRIPTURE REFERENCES

1 John 1:9	Ephesians 2:10
Luke 17:21	Ephesians 1:19,20
Colossians 1:29	Psalm 27:1
Hebrews 13:5	1 John 4:4
Romans 3:31	Proverbs 29:25
Joshua 1:5	Philippians 4:13
2 Timothy 1:7	

—40—

RESISTING PEER PRESSURE

Father, please help me to be strong and not to give in to negative peer pressure. I trust You to keep peer pressure from becoming so overwhelming that I can't stand up against it. You will show me how to escape temptation's power so I can bear up patiently against it.

I resist the lust of the flesh, the lust of the eyes, and the pride of life. I strive for integrity, faith, love, peace, and holiness in all of my relationships.

I know that You love me and want the best for me. I will not follow the plans and purposes of the ungodly, or stand submissive and inactive in the path where sinners walk. I delight in the law of the Lord and on Your law I will habitually meditate. My security and self-esteem are in You, and I do not seek the approval of others to feel secure.

I will walk as a companion with wise men and I shall be wise. Your nature abides in me — Your principle of life abides permanently within me, and I cannot habitually practice sinning because I am born of God.

In Jesus' name I pray. Amen.

SCRIPTURE REFERENCES

Psalm 1:1,2 TLB	1 Thessalonians 4:4
Psalm 27:1	1 Timothy 4:12
Proverbs 11:3 KJV	2 Timothy 2:22
Proverbs 13:20 AMP	Hebrews 4:15
1 Corinthians 10:13 TLB	Hebrews 12:14 KJV
2 Corinthians 6:16-18	1 John 2:16 KJV
Ephesians 6:10	1 John 3:9 AMP
Philippians 4:13	

—41—

FORGIVENESS WHEN YOU SIN

Father, I am sorry that I have sinned against You. I believe that You are compassionate, slow to anger, and filled with mercy and love, so I run right to You and not away from You. I confess my sin of _____, and ask Your forgiveness. I don't deceive myself by trying to say that I have not sinned.

Father, I repent and turn from my sin. I determine with Your help to make the necessary changes in my life. Thank You for forgiving me and giving me a pure heart and renewing a right spirit within me. I am blessed because You have removed my transgressions from me as far as the east is from the west. You have removed the weight of sin and lifted the burden of guilt that have been weighing upon me. So by faith I receive my forgiveness.

In Jesus' name I pray. Amen.

SCRIPTURE REFERENCES

Psalm 32:1,2	Philippians 2:5,13
Psalm 51:10,17	Colossians 2:13,14 AMP
Psalm 103:2-4,8,11-13 AMP	Hebrews 1:9
Proverbs 28:13	Hebrews 4:16
Acts 26:20	Hebrews 12:1 KJV
Romans 6:13,14	1 John 1:8-10

— 42 —

ABSTINENCE FROM PREMARITAL SEX

Father, in view of Your mercy, I offer my body as a living sacrifice, holy and pleasing to You — this is my spiritual act of worship. I will not copy the sexual behavior and customs of this world.

Sexual sin is never right. No other sin affects the body as this one does. This sin is against my own body. My body is not meant for sexual immorality, but for You, and You for the body.

My body is the temple of the Holy Spirit. I am not my own, but You have bought me with a great price. I use every part of my body to bring glory to You, because my body belongs to You.

In Jesus' name I pray. Amen.

SCRIPTURE REFERENCES

Psalm 119:9	1 Corinthians 10:13
Romans 6:13,14	1 Thessalonians 4:4
Romans 8:5,6	1 Thessalonians 5:22,23 KJV
Romans 12:1,2 TLB	James 1:22
1 Corinthians 6:18-20 TLB	1 Peter 1:18,19
1 Corinthians 9:22 TLB	

—43—

ALCOHOL/DRUG/TOBACCO ADDICTION

Father, in the mighty name of Jesus, I come boldly to Your throne of grace that I may obtain mercy and find grace to help in my time of need. I believe that You can deliver me and protect me from every evil.

Lord, I want to be free from alcohol/drugs/tobacco, but I can't do it alone; I need Your help. I believe Your Word, and that truth will set me free, because since Jesus has made me free, I am free indeed. I need Your help to overcome temptation. Give me the grace I need to walk in the Spirit, so I won't fulfill the lusts of the flesh. Help me to control my thoughts so that I will obey Your Word. Keep me from willful sins. May they not rule over me. I desire to be pleasing in Your sight.

Father, You are faithful. You will not allow me to be tempted beyond my powers of endurance. In every temptation You will always show me a way out. I determine not to go to the wrong types of parties or places that will make it easier to give in to alcohol/drugs/tobacco.

I will renew my mind by reading Your Word so that I can change the way I think and be set free from bad habits and from the lies that I have been believing. I believe that You can even change my desires, Father, when I delight myself in You. Thank You that I have been freed from my sin by the blood of Jesus.

Thank You for forgiving me and for forgetting the sins of my past. I look to You for a great, new future. It is a new day! I am a new person — I am a new creation in Christ Jesus.

Thank You, Lord, for a life free from addictions. Please guide me to a godly counselor, friend, or support group. Thank You that You are giving me good habits where I once had bad habits.

In Jesus' name I pray. Amen.

SCRIPTURE REFERENCES

Psalm 19:13	1 Corinthians 15:33,34
Psalm 37:4-6 KJV	2 Corinthians 5:17
Psalm 103:11-14	Galatians 5:18-21
Isaiah 43:18,19	Ephesians 5:18
Jeremiah 29:11	Philippians 1:10
John 8:32,36 KJV	Philippians 4:8
Romans 6:23	2 Timothy 4:18
Romans 13:14 KJV	Hebrews 4:14-16
1 Corinthians 5:11	James 4:7
1 Corinthians 9:25-27	2 Peter 2:9
1 Corinthians 10:13 Phillips	1 John 1:7 KJV
1 Corinthians 15:3 Beck	

—44—

WHEN YOU LOSE SOMETHING

Father, I come boldly to Your throne of grace in my time of need. I ask in the name of Jesus that You help me to find _____ (name the object that is lost). Thank You that You perfect that which concerns me. Holy Spirit, help me to remember where I was when I last saw or handled it.

Father, if I lost _____ due to my carelessness, please forgive me and help me to be more diligent in managing those things that You have so freely given me. I desire to make good use of everything I have.

You have blessed me with all spiritual blessings in Christ Jesus. Even the money I earn is a blessing from You. I commit the care of this situation to You, for I know that You care for me.

Because You are Lord over all of my life, Father, You will straighten my course and direct my feet. If someone deliberately took _____, I forgive that person, and pray that the Holy Spirit will convince him/her of sin, of righteousness, and of judgment and will bring him/her to repentance.

Father, if You desire that I consider this loss as a gift, I do so in the name of Jesus and thank You for the return on it.

Thank You, Father, for guiding me and providing me with the answer.

In Jesus' name I pray. Amen.

SCRIPTURE REFERENCES

Psalm 37:23   Luke 6:38

Psalm 73:24   Luke 8:17

Psalm 138:8 KJV   John 14:26

Proverbs 2:6-8	John 16:7,8 AMP
Proverbs 3:5-7 AMP	1 Corinthians 2:10
Proverbs 12:27 TLB	Ephesians 1:3
Proverbs 16:3	Hebrews 4:16
Ecclesiastes 5:19	James 1:5
Isaiah 30:21	1 Peter 5:7 KJV
Matthew 10:26	2 Peter 3:9 KJV

—45—

WHEN SOMEONE LIES ABOUT YOU

Father, I come before You in the name of Jesus. Lies have been spoken against me, and I feel hurt, betrayed, and humiliated. I confess the anger and hatred that I feel toward those who have spread these rumors. I know that Your Word says that I am to pray for those who persecute me, and that I am to love my enemies. These negative emotions keep getting in the way of my desire to obey Your Word.

I choose to give You these tormenting emotions that are robbing me of peace, love, joy, my study time, and my sleep. Help me to release these agonies to You by forgiving those who have wronged me. You and I know the truth, but the stares and whispers of former friends still hurt. I feel cut off even from those who say they love me.

Jesus, You were shunned and forsaken by Your friends, and You understand the pain that I feel.

Father, I know that I cannot control the behavior of others, but with the help of the Holy Spirit I can control mine. You said that no weapon formed against me will prevail, and that every tongue that rises against me in judgment I shall show to be in the wrong. I do believe that You keep me secretly in Your pavilion from the strife of tongues, from the lies that could cause me to behave in a spiteful and revengeful manner. You have given me the spirit of self-control, and I desire to walk before those who have hurt me in a manner that is pleasing to You, for You are the glory and the lifter of my head.

Lies endure for only a season, but truth endures forever. I thank You, Father, that You always cause me to triumph in Christ Jesus and that You have given me favor like a shield with all those who are involved.

In Jesus' name I pray. Amen.

SCRIPTURE REFERENCES

Psalm 3:3 KJV	Isaiah 53:3
Psalm 5:12	Isaiah 54:17 TLB
Psalm 25:20,21	Matthew 5:44
Psalm 26:1	Matthew 6:14,15
Psalm 34:20 KJV	John 8:44
Psalm 37:1	2 Corinthians 2:14 KJV
Psalm 101:6-8	Ephesians 4:29
Proverbs 12:19 AMP	2 Timothy 1:7 AMP
Proverbs 21:23	James 1:19

—46—

WHEN OTHERS MAKE
FUN OF YOU

Father, I come to You in the name that is above all
other names — the name of Jesus. You hold me in the
palm of Your hand, and Your name is a strong tower
that I can run into and be safe even when people make
fun of me. I admit that their words really hurt me.

I desire to be accepted by my classmates, but I long
to obey You and follow Your commandments. I know
that Jesus was tempted just as I am, but He didn't give
in to sin or hate. Please give me Your mercy and grace
to deal with this situation. I look to You for my
comfort; You are a true friend at all times.

Thank You for never leaving me alone or rejecting
me. I make a decision to forgive the people who have
made fun of me. I ask You to work this forgiveness in
my heart. I submit to You and reject the disappoint-

ment and anger that have attempted to consume me. Specifically right now I forgive _____.

I ask You to cause this situation to accommodate itself for good in my life. I know that when I am tempted to compromise my Christian beliefs, You give me the strength to be the person that You created me to be with assurance and confidence.

Father, I will resist the temptation to strike back in anger. I purpose to love _____ with the love of Jesus in me. Mercy and truth are written upon the tablets of my heart; therefore, You will cause me to find favor and understanding with all my teachers and classmates. Keep me from self-righteousness that I may walk in Your righteousness. Thank You for sending and giving me friends who will stand by me and for teaching me how to guard my heart with all diligence.

I declare that in the midst of all these things I am more than a conqueror through Jesus Who loves me.

In Jesus' name I pray. Amen.

SCRIPTURE REFERENCES

Psalm 1:1-3	Romans 1:16
Psalm 31:20 KJV	Romans 5:5
Psalm 119:165	Romans 8:28,37
Proverbs 3:3 AMP	1 Corinthians 4:4
Proverbs 3:4 KJV	1 Corinthians 10:13
Proverbs 4:23 KJV	Ephesians 4:32
Proverbs 16:4 AMP	Philippians 2:9
Proverbs 17:17	Colossians 1:10,11
Proverbs 18:10,24 KJV	Hebrews 4:15,16
Isaiah 49:16	Hebrews 13:5
Matthew 5:10-12	1 John 3:13
Matthew 6:14,15	

—47—

WHEN YOU FEEL LONELY
OR UNLOVED

Father, when other people leave me and I feel unloved, I am thankful that You will never, ever leave me alone or reject me. You are a help for me in this time of loneliness. I know that Your angels are all around me.

You are my God. I know that You love me. Jesus even gave His life for me. I am a born-again Christian. Jesus lives in my heart, and I am on my way to heaven. That is plenty to be thankful for. So I won't allow myself to be discouraged or feel sorry for myself. I choose to think only on those things that are pure, and holy, and good, even when I am alone.

Although I may feel alone, I know that I am not alone, for Your Word says that there is nothing that can separate me from the love of Christ. I will come out on top of every circumstance through Jesus' love.

In Jesus' name I pray. Amen.

SCRIPTURE REFERENCES

Deuteronomy 31:8	Romans 8:35,37
1 Samuel 30:6	Romans 10:9,10
Psalm 34:7	Romans 12:21
Psalm 37:4	Ephesians 4:31,32
Psalm 46:1	Ephesians 5:1,2
John 3:16	Philippians 4:8
John 16:32	Hebrews 13:5,6
Romans 5:5	

—48—

A BROKEN HOME

Father, Your Word says that when my Mom or my Dad forsake me, You will receive me. I know that I am accepted in Jesus.

I get frustrated thinking about what has happened to my parents and family, but I look to You as my help. You sent Jesus to mend our hurts and heal our broken hearts. Jesus will never leave us comfortless or without help.

Help me by Your Holy Spirit to be strong. I will not allow myself to become bitter or to speak bad or evil words about anyone, even though I may feel like it. I desire to be kind, loving, and forgiving, just like Jesus. I am going to think only on the things that are good, pure, true, clean, and holy. If I am angry, I will not sin. I will continue to look to You for help.

I ask for supernatural peace to keep me from being worried or afraid. Thank You for giving me and my family a peace that is more wonderful than anyone can imagine.

I don't understand all that is going on with my family, so I pray that You will show my parents and family the right decisions to make. I pray that they will realize the love that You have for them and that You will be their friend also.

Show the unsaved members of my family that they need to ask Jesus to be their Savior. Send someone across their path from whom they can receive counsel, and help them to forgive each other so there will be a healing in their relationships.

Father, although this situation seems hopeless, there is nothing that is impossible for You. You sent Jesus so that we could have life to the fullest. I know that each person has his or her own will and can choose to follow You or reject You. Although I really love all my family, I will not allow them to drag me down into depression, discouragement, despair, hatred, or strife, because Your joy is my strength. I know that this situation is not my fault.

I pray and ask that the fruit of the Spirit — love, joy, peace, humility, meekness, and self-control — will replace all evil works. Thank You that I can be a light and a hope for my family.

Father, thank You for moving in my family and keeping all of us from harm or evil. I say that this is a new day and that You are doing a new thing in my family.

In Jesus' name I pray. Amen.

SCRIPTURE REFERENCES

Nehemiah 8:10	John 10:10
Psalm 27:10	John 14:16-18,27
Psalm 33:20	Acts 16:31
Psalm 147:3	Galatians 5:19-23 AMP

Proverbs 3:5,6	Ephesians 1:6 KJV
Isaiah 43:19	Ephesians 3:14-19
Isaiah 61:1-3	Ephesians 4:26,27,29-32
Luke 1:37	Philippians 4:6-8
Luke 4:18,19	

—49—

ABUSE*

Physical and Sexual Abuse:

Heavenly Father, thank You that I can run to You for safety and protection and that You are my shield from abuse. I am the apple of Your eye, and am engraved on the palms of Your hands. I refuse to blame myself for this personal invasion. I have not brought this behavior upon myself.

In the name of Jesus, I forgive _____ who has betrayed me with smooth words while in his/her heart was evil intent. His/her words were sweet, but underneath were drawn swords. Give me the courage to report my situation to the right godly counselor. I cast my cares upon You and You will sustain me through all my deliverance. You will not allow me to slip or fall.

---

* See "Protection."

Father, because You are my shield and fortress, I can be protected. I will not fear him who can destroy only the body — who can't touch my soul. It is Your Word that defends my soul. I know that You love me and that nothing can separate me from Your love. You will never leave me alone or reject me.

Help me to keep Your joy. I will not allow any feelings of bitterness, hatred, resentment, or evil to control my life. I release these feelings in Jesus' name and allow myself to be healed from their sting.

In Jesus' name I pray. Amen.

Verbal Abuse:

Heavenly Father, thank You that I can run to You for safety and protection and that You are my shield from verbal abuse. I am the apple of Your eye, and am engraved in the palms of Your hands. I refuse to blame myself for this personal invasion. I have not brought this behavior upon myself. The bitter words spoken against me have been like arrows shot from ambush at my child-like innocence.

I am trusting in You alone, O Lord. Rescue me from those who would destroy me with their words. Thank You for Your favor. Save me just because You are so kind. Hide me in the shelter of Your presence and keep me safe from accusing tongues.

Father, I thank You that Your Word assures me that Your intent is to prosper me and not to harm me. Your plans for me give me hope and a future.

I will encourage myself in You, seeing myself chosen before the foundation of the world and accepted in the beloved. I stand before You, covered with Your love. I belong to Your dearly beloved Son, overflowing in His kindness towards me.

Father, You understand me. I extend kindness and forgiveness to those who have abused me verbally.

In Jesus' name I pray. Amen.

SCRIPTURE REFERENCES

1 Samuel 30:6 KJV	Matthew 5:44
2 Samuel 22:3	Matthew 6:14
Nehemiah 8:10	Matthew 10:28
Psalm 17:4,8	Luke 4:18
Psalm 31:1-24	Romans 5:19
Psalm 55:20-22 AMP	Romans 8:35-39
Psalm 64:1-10	2 Corinthians 5:21
Psalm 147:3,6	2 Corinthians 10:3-5
Isaiah 40:8	Ephesians 1:3-6 KJV
Isaiah 41:13	Philippians 4:8
Isaiah 49:16	Hebrews 13:5
Jeremiah 29:11	James 4:7
Jeremiah 30:17	1 Peter 2:24
Joel 2:25	Revelation 12:10

ABOUT THE AUTHOR

Germaine Griffin Copeland, founder and president of Word Ministries, Inc., is the author of the *Prayers That Avail Much*® family of books. Her writings provide scriptural prayer instruction to help you pray more effec-  tively for those things that concern you and your family and for other prayer assignments. Her teachings on prayer, the personal growth on the intercessor, emotional healing and related subjects have brought understanding, hope, healing and liberty to the discouraged and emotionally wounded. She is a woman of prayer and praise whose highest form of worship is the study of God's Word. Her greatest desire is to know God.

Word Ministries, Inc. is a prayer and teaching ministry. Germaine believes that God has called her to teach the practical application of the Word of Truth for successful victorious living. After years of searching diligently for truth and trying again and again to come out of depression, she decided that she was a mistake. Out of the depths of despair she called upon the name of the Lord, and the light of God's presence invaded the room where she was sitting.

It was in that moment that she experienced the warmth of God's love; old things passed away, and she felt brand new. She discovered a motivation for living — life had a purpose. Living in the presence of God she has found unconditional love and acceptance, healing for crippled emotions, contentment that overcomes depression, peace in the midst of adverse circumstances and grace for developing healthy relationships. The ongoing process of transformation evolved into praying for others, and the prayer of intercession became her prayer focus.

Germaine is the daughter of Reverend A. H. "Buck" Griffin and the late Donnis Brock Griffin. She and her husband, Everette, have four children, and their prayer assignments increase as more grandchildren and great grandchildren are born. Germaine and Everette reside in Sandy Springs, a suburb of Atlanta, Georgia.

You may contact Word Ministries by writing:

Word Ministries, Inc.

38 Sloan Street

Roswell, Georgia 30075

or calling 770-518-1065

www.prayers.org

*Please include your testimonies
and praise reports when you write.*

MISSION STATEMENT
WORD MINISTRIES, INC.

To motivate individuals to spiritual growth

and emotional wholeness,

encouraging them to become more deeply

and intimately acquainted

with the Father God

as they pray prayers that avail much.

OTHER BOOKS BY
GERMAINE COPELAND

A Call to Prayer

The Road God Walks

Prayers That Avail Much Commemorative Gift Edition

Prayers That Avail Much Commemorative Leather Edition

Prayers That Avail Much for Business

Prayers That Avail Much Volume 1

Prayers That Avail Much Volume 1 — mass market edition

Prayers That Avail Much Volume 2

Prayers That Avail Much Volume 2 — mass market edition

Prayers That Avail Much Volume 3

Prayers That Avail Much Volume 3 — mass market edition

Prayers That Avail Much for Men

Prayers That Avail Much for Women

Prayers That Avail Much for Mothers — hardbound

Prayers That Avail Much for Mothers
mass market edition

Prayers That Avail Much for Teens — hardbound

Prayers That Avail Much for Teens — mass market edition

Prayers That Avail Much for Kids

Prayers That Avail Much for Kids — Book 2

Prayers That Avail Much for the Workplace

Oraciones Con Poder — Prayers That Avail Much
(Spanish Edition)

Available from your local bookstore.

HARRISON HOUSE

Tulsa, OK 74153

PRAYER OF SALVATION

A born-again, committed relationship with God is the key to the victorious life. Jesus laid down His life and rose again so that we could spend eternity with Him in heaven and experience His absolute best on earth. If you would like to receive Jesus into your life in order to become born-again, pray this prayer from your heart:

Heavenly Father, I come to You admitting that I am a sinner. Right now, I choose to turn away from sin, and I ask You to cleanse me of all unrighteousness. I believe that Your Son, Jesus, died on the cross to take away my sins. I also believe that He rose again from the dead so that I might be justified and made righteous through faith in Him. I call upon the name of Jesus Christ to be the Savior and Lord of my life. Jesus, I choose to follow You, and ask that You fill me with the power of the Holy Spirit. I declare that right now, I am a child of God. I am free from sin, and full of the righteousness of God. I am saved in Jesus' name, Amen.

If you prayed this prayer to receive Jesus Christ as your Savior for the first time, please contact us on the web at <u>www.harrisonhouse</u>.com to receive a free book.

Or you may write to us at

Harrison House Publishers
P.O. Box 35035
Tulsa, Oklahoma 74153

Please include your prayer requests and comments when you write.

THE HARRISON HOUSE VISION

Proclaiming the truth and the power

Of the Gospel of Jesus Christ

With excellence;

Challenging Christians to

Live victoriously,

Grow spiritually,

Know God intimately.